Lose Weight
Permanently
and Naturally

Lose Weight
Permanently
and Naturally

Dr. Bruce Goldberg

GOLD

Published by
Bruce Goldberg, Inc.
4300 Natoma Ave.
Woodland Hills, CA 91364
Telephone: (800) KARMA-4-U or
FAX: (818) 704-9189
Email: drbg@sbcglobal.net
Web Site:
www.drbrucegoldberg.com

Printed in the United States of America

ISBN 1-57968-015-1

Publisher's Note: This publication is designed to provide accurate and informative information in regard to the subject matter covered. It is sold or distributed with the understanding that the publisher and author is not engaged in rendering legal, accounting, or other professional service. If legal advice or other expert assistance is required, the services of a competent professional person in a consultation capacity should be sought.

CONTENTS

About the Author

Dr. Bruce Goldberg holds a B.A. degree in Biology and Chemistry, is a Doctor of Dental Surgery, and has an M.S. degree in Counseling Psychology. He retired from dentistry in 1989, and has concentrated on his hypnotherapy practice in Los Angeles. Dr. Goldberg was trained by the American Society of Clinical Hypnosis in the techniques and clinical applications of hypnosis in 1975.

Dr. Goldberg has interviewed on the Donahue, *Oprah, Leeza, Joan Rivers, Regis, ABC Radio, Art Bell, Tom Snyder, Jerry Springer, Jenny Jones,* and *Montel Williams* shows; by *CNN, CBS News, NBC,* and many others.

Through lectures, television and radio appearances, and news*paper articles, including interviews in Time* the *Los Angeles Times, USA Today,* and the *Washington Post,* he has conducted more than 35,000 past-life regressions and future-life progressions since 1974, helping thousands of patients empower themselves through these techniques. His CDs, cassette tapes and DVDs teach people self-hypnosis, and guide them into past and future lives and time travel. He gives lectures and seminars on hypnosis, regression and progression therapy, time travel, and conscious dying; he is also a consultant to corporations, attorneys, and the local and network media. His first edition of *The Search for Grace,* was made into a television movie by CBS. His third book, the award winning *Soul Healing,* is a classic on alternative medicine and psychic empowerment. *Past Lives—Future Lives* is Dr.

Goldberg's international bestseller and is the first book written on future lives (progression hypnotherapy).

Dr. Goldberg distributes CDs, cassette tapes, and DVDs to teach people self-hypnosis and to guide them into past and future lives and time travel. For information on self-hypnosis tapes, speaking engagements, or private sessions, Dr. Goldberg can be contacted directly by writing to:

Bruce Goldberg, D.D.S., M.S.
4300 Natoma Avenue, Woodland Hills, CA 91364
Telephone: (800) Karma-4-U or (800) 527-6248
Fax: (818) 704-9189
email: drbg@sbcglobal.net
Website: www.drbrucegoldberg.com

Please include a self-addressed, stamped envelope with your letter.

OTHER BOOKS BY
DR. BRUCE GOLDBERG

Past Live, Future Lives
Soul Healing
The Search for Grace: A Documented Case of Murder and Reincarnation
Peaceful Transition: The Art of Conscious Dying and the Liberation of the Soul
New Age Hypnosis
Karmic Capitalism: A Spiritual Approach to Financial Independence
Unleash Your Psychic Powers
Look Younger and Live Longer: Add 25 to 50 Quality Years to Your Life Naturally
Protected by the Light: The Complete Book of Psychic Self Defense
Time Travelers from Our Future: A Fifth Dimension Odyssey
Astral Voyages: Mastering the art of Interdimensional Travel
Custom Design Your Own Destiny
Self-Hypnosis: Easy Ways to Hypnotize Your Problems Away
Dream Your Problems Away: Heal Yourself While You Sleep
Egypt: An Extraterrestrial and Time Traveler Experiment
Past Lives, Future Lives Revealed

INTRODUCTION

Being overweight can cost you your marriage, job and health. It destroys your self-image, attracts criticism to your discipline, and is commonly associated with depression. Weight issues are a very serious problem that decreases both the quality and quantity of life.

Most people with weight problems have tried methods to lose their excess weight. They fail, and fail often. The reason for this failure is that the cause for overeating was not removed.

The cause is not glandular, a dysfunctional childhood or even "fork and mouth disease." One has to look at our very being to seek the etiology of a disorder that affects over half of Americans.

No gland can create fat. A slow metabolism will still properly remove excess protein, carbohydrates and fats from our body. Inner, disturbing emotions such as anxiety and depression are far more causative than any other factor that is improperly labeled today.

Until we learn to cope with the difficulties and stresses of our lives, the pattern of utilizing food as a tranquilizer or diversion will remain etched in our society. This book will show you why dieting is both unnecessary and one of the causes of overeating.

I will present methods, such as self-hypnosis, that override the will power and reprogram our subconscious mind to eliminate the true causes of overeating. You will learn never to count calories, diet, fast and how to live a healthier lifestyle that will make your weight loss permanent and natural.

Other benefits you will obtain from reading this book are:

- How to incorporate easy to do exercises into your life.
- How to create a leaner mind set by concentrating on how you lead your life, not how much you weigh.

- How to develop more balanced eating habits.
- How to read food labels and eliminate high-fat foods from your shopping list.
- How to live healthier and naturally maintain your ideal weight.
- How to induce and use self-hypnosis to empower yourself in all aspects of your life.
- How to raise your level of spiritual growth while you lose weight permanently.

What this book will not teach you are the following dysfunctional behaviors:

- Obsessing about your weight.
- Setting unrealistic standards of perfection.
- Equating happiness with weight loss.
- Developing guilt feelings about food.
- Procrastinating life style changes that allow you to attain your weight and overall health goals.
- Counting calories, inches and pounds.
- Forming an opinion of yourself by how much you weigh.

HOW TO USE THIS BOOK

This book contains dozens of exercises specifically designed to train you to lose excess weight and keep it off. It doesn't matter what your background is.

You can accept or reject any of the principles and concepts presented here. Empowerment is vital. I stress that in my hypnotherapy practice and in my personal life as well. If you become rigid and stuck in your views, you become trapped by your beliefs. You are no longer empowered because you are no longer free.

Always use your judgment and free will in trying these exercises. Use the ones you feel comfortable with and ignore the others. These exercises are all perfectly safe and have been tested for over 25 years. You can always create your own exercises from these models.

Read each exercise through to become familiar with it. Use the relaxation techniques given or your own and practice the exercises. You may practice alone or with others. Feel free to make tapes of these exercises. Read the scripts slowly and leave enough space on your tape to experience each part of the procedure.

If you experience difficulty with an exercise, do not become frustrated. Some techniques are quite advanced and you may not be ready for all of them. At another time, return to the ones you could not successfully work with.

Practice these trance states when you have time and when you are relaxed. Be patient. It takes time to master trance states and to become accustomed to this new and wonderful world. No one way is *the* right way to experience a trance. Your body may feel light, or it may feel heavy; you may feel as if you are dreaming;

your eyelids may flutter; or your body can become cooler or warmer. All these possible responses are perfectly safe.

Your initial practice sessions should be as long as you need, since you are unfamiliar with the techniques. As you become more proficient, you will be able to shorten these sessions. Some days nothing may seem to work. Try not to become discouraged. Remember, other days will be more fruitful. Always work at your own pace with an open mind.

CHAPTER 1

LOSING WEIGHT SPIRITUALLY-THE BIG

PICTURE

I'm sure most people have some idea of how to stay healthy by a combination of diet, exercise and rest. We may understand the psychological factors that exert an influence upon our physical body. Many of us lack a clear understanding of how the nonphysical, spiritual energies in life can affect our health, and our ability to lose weight.

The spiritual energies that continually interact with our physical body dramatically influence our bodies, our thoughts, and our emotions. We don't really understand these forces because they are usually hidden from our ordinary awareness. The purpose of this book is to help bring the hidden spiritual energies into a clearer focus so that we may consciously draw upon them to create emotional, mental, and physical functions in our lives that will allow us to lose weight permanently and naturally.

Before I present detailed information about diet, exercise and mind-body natural methods to assist you in your quest for permanent weight loss, a discussion of just how spiritual growth can make this a reality is in order. I like to refer to this as a global assessment, or the big picture, in natural and permanent weight loss.

SPIRITUALITY AS THE BIG PICTURE

Spirituality has been receiving increased attention from both health care providers and consumers. Recent literature provides exploration of and some clarity in understanding and its relationship to health. Spirit is understood to be both the source of and a manifestation of one's spirituality.

Spirituality is a unifying force, manifested in the Self, and reflected in one's being, one's knowing, and one's doing. It is expressed and experienced in the context of caring connections with oneself, others, nature, our Higher Self (the perfect component of our soul) and God. The key elements of this view of spirituality are the Self and connections. The Self reflects an unfolding life journey that embodies who one is, what and how one knows, and what one does, as well as one's source of strength and meaning. Connections are those attachments and relationships that link Self to others, nature, the Higher Self and God. Spirituality relates to an inner knowing and source of strength reflected in one's being, one's knowing, and one's doing.

The reason many of us fail to maintain our proper weight is that the energy of desire is intimately woven with the creative power of the soul. The eternal life force that we call the soul gives rise to our creativity, strength, will, and other capacities that flow from our soul into our personality. When we desire something so intensely (like fattening foods), that feeling of desire stirs up the very powerful soul energies within us that have been given to us so that we can create, act, and accomplish in order to fulfill our purpose in the physical world.

Those individuals who are susceptible to immediate gratification behaviors have created a climate that encourages the instant fulfillment of physical desires. A certain numbing results from this process of eating, ingesting alcohol and drugs, and sexual highs through continual fulfillment. For example, if you go forth each day seeking only to fulfill the desire to eat food, to fill yourself with the pleasure of taste and other pleasant sensations of eating, and that is all you do each day, then, after a while, the intense experience of the joy of eating begins to diminish. Then, you attempt to eat more, or you may try to have more intense experiences by eating foods with different tastes. Unintentionally, you set up a cycle in which your search for fulfillment is based upon an experience of satiation, or numbness in your present fulfillment.

A far more spiritual approach is to create a desire to be emotionally fulfilled in profound inner ways that involve love, and that bring about the experience of purpose and meaning in life. Compulsive eating problems can be eliminated by focusing on the following three areas: (1) learning to bring joy into all other areas of your life outside of the eating experience; (2) learning to open your heart to love yourself and those around you; and (3) healing your fears by accessing your Higher Self. Successfully accomplishing these three goals will bring you the confidence and trust in your own unlimited capacities of strength, creativity, and love that will help you release the desire to substitute addictive behaviors for the true joy and wonders of life.

Another benefit from this suggested regimen is that it frees you to utilize your Higher Self to create your body image without interference from negative, personality patterns associated with poor eating habits and low self image. By daily committing yourself to heal your negative thoughts, feelings, attitude and beliefs, you begin a change in your personality that fosters any goal humanly possible.

ESTABLISHING A SPIRITUAL FOUNDATION

When you are kind to others and assist them in times of need, you bring up from inside your very soul a joy and fulfillment that will make your desires to lose weight permanently far easier to attain. A harmonious inner life of thought and feeling will assist you in making intelligent choices about the physical aspects of your life, such as what you eat, how you exercise your body, how you relate to other human beings, and other interactions with the physical world that you will have daily.

The more you heal your soul and establish this spiritual foundation, the more calmness, happiness, joy, and understanding you
have in your attitude towards food and eating, and towards life.
Now the body is free to function perfectly in the way that it takes
in the food, assimilates it, and eliminates its waste.

The opposite is also true. Unhealed negative attitudes towards
food, and towards life, over a period of time, can interfere with the
way your body uses whatever food you put into it. Your attitudes
about life in general will affect your eating. If you eat when you are
depressed, the food may not digest properly, and it might not be
fully utilized by your body. If you have constant fear, doubt, and
worry throughout your life, then there will be disturbances set up
in the digestive processes of your body, which can eventually bring
about challenges to your health. This combination may result in
the overeating of unhealthy foods and weight problems.

What I have observed over the years in my Los Angeles hypnotherapy practice is that those patients who exhibit a more spiritual
love of themselves, as opposed to ego, tend to be drawn to foods that
are healthy. They will not usually develop such strong desires to eat
foods in the extreme ranges. This is not to say that if you like foods at
the extreme ranges then you do not love yourself. My observation is
simply a generalization that applies to the majority of the more than
11,000 individual patients I have worked with since 1974.

If you can use your creativity daily to bring forth all of the
energies of love that live within you, then you can manifest a strength
and forcefulness in your body, emotions, mind, and your soul to
create and attain any goal you desire. We all possess this ability to
create the experience of love inside us at any moment, and that
experience will bring the energies of love into our conscious life.
There is nothing that can prevent you from using our ability to
create love, except our own ego.

The first step in learning to create love in any moment is be-
lieving that you have the ability to do it. It is only your own lack of
belief in that ability and an unwillingness to use it that can prevent this creation of love.

It will not benefit you to try to relive your negative experiences because you are frightened of the pain of them. If you attempt to bring forth your capacity to create love, motivated by a fear of your own painful experiences, you will only eventually create more fear.

By working honestly and lovingly each day with your negative patterns of thought and emotion, you can use your ability to step back from the complexity of your inner reality and turn your attention to creating love at that moment.

There are two modes of subjective experience. The first mode is the inner experience mode-living intensely inside your inner experience, and being caught up in your experience. In that mode, you are the creator of your experience.

Mode two is the observer or other experience mode-stepping back from the intensity of your experience to observe what you are experiencing. In this mode, you are the responder to your experience. This allows you to step back from your experience by creating a loving detachment from your subjectivity of the moment, not by numbering your feelings. This detachment is a temporary mode. A continuous use of this mode could result in a loss of intensity of your subjective experience. However, it will be necessary to use this second mode in a limited way in order to fully exercise your capacity to create love at any moment.

This method can be applied after you have learned to make this inner shift in your thoughts and feelings of the moment. Then, whenever you desire, you can enter that deeper awareness of your Higher Self, and, from within that deepened experience, you can create feelings of warmth, harmony, and love within yourself. If you attain that capacity and develop it, gradually you will learn that you can also use this ability to come forth to help others create love in their lives.

When you joyfully choose to align with the eternal energies of life, and you choose to make them the center of your life on Earth, then you bring a magnificence and perfection into your experience that is a true expression of the Higher Self.

CARING FOR THE SOUL

Thomas Moore suggests that living artfully is necessary for care of
the soul. What he refers to as requirements of living artfully, pausing, taking time, and mindfulness or paying attention—reflect
common themes found in these various traditions. Pausing, which
is an antithetical stance in our busy world, gives time for stopping,
reflecting, and taking in what has happened and is happening
within and around us. Savoring, appreciating, being still, wonder-
ing, and reconsidering are a few of the opportunities presented by
pausing.

Taking time for self and with persons, relationships, and things
enable us to come to know them and be known by them. By doing
this, our connections grow stronger, deeper, more intimate. Our
spirits are nourished, stretched, and shaped, even when relationships are fraught with struggle. Taking time and being careful as
we are involved with persons and things deepens our understanding and appreciation of them.[1]

Being mindful and paying attention are aspects of pausing
and taking time. This mindfulness and attention helps one to know
when to pause and when to take time, as well as how to spend
time in nourishing the spirit. We will discuss mindfulness again in
chapter 6. The purpose of attention is to produce awareness and
thereby reach or uncover the awakened state of mind. Paying attention is the essence of true spirituality. Most spiritual practices
are different ways of helping one learn to pay attention.

Centering is an important step in the process of being in touch
with one's spirit. Centering focuses one's attention and opens one's
awareness. There are a number of ways to get centered. Just about
every Eastern and Western spiritual tradition proposes its own favorite ways of centering, such as: counting the breath, focusing on the
breathing process, repeating a ritual movement, reciting sacred words,
chanting, dancing, creating an imaginative scene, and so on.

Any experience in which one is paying attention can be a time
of centering because it opens one to being fully present and aware

in that moment. Such experiences can take many forms, and an individual may discover more than one path to centering. The important choice is the commitment to increasing attention and awareness through the practice of spiritual disciplines such as prayer and meditation, hypnosis and through recognition of the spirit-enhancing opportunities in ordinary activities of life such as cooking, walking, and playing.

Deep experiences of spirit come through connections, in the midst of community and in solitude. Experiences of the Self and solitude are not separate from or unrelated to experiences of community and connection. All are parts of one's wholeness. Experiences of the Self that may involve solitude in the process of caring for self include prayer/meditation/hypnosis, body-work/movement/ sensing, rest/waiting/leisure, ritual, and creative expression/the arts.

Experiences of connections that are significant to the care of the spirit include connections to persons, communities and to the physical environment. The rich connections of life in community offer great potential for nurturing one's spirit. It is important to plan time with others who, in many different ways, nurture and affirm one's being. In workplaces, homes, communities, and the larger world, persons who are able to be present, to hear stories of deep pain and joy, and share the struggles and triumphs of one's journey, shape one's life.

Using gifts of creativity gives expression to the soul. Weaving, sketching, sculpting, writing, photography, and listening to or making music are some ways of caring for the soul. Enjoying and pondering plays, music, literature, movies, and art are avenues of learning about and nurture for the spirit. The world around us offers many opportunities for connecting to spirit. The interdependence of all of creation becomes increasingly clear as the wisdom of ancient traditions and recent scientific findings remind us. Nature gives to us through our senses—the smell of flowers, the taste of herbs, the feel of sand between our toes, the sound of waves breaking, the sight of geese flying overhead. For many, the outdoors is a sacred space that calls to and nourishes spirit.

Leaning against a tree, wading in a stream, watching a small critter, and planting a garden are among many paths to spirit.

Consider the following reflective questions and ask these of yourself in assessing, evaluating, and increasing awareness of the spiritual process in yourself.

- What gives your life meaning?
- Do you have a sense of purpose in life?
- How hopeful are you about your ability to reach and maintain your ideal weight?
- Will you be able to make changes in your life to lose weight permanently and naturally?
- Are you motivated to lose weight without dieting or resorting to artificial aids?
- How do you feel about yourself right now?
- How do you feel when you have a true sense of yourself?
- Do you pursue things of personal interest?
- What do you do to show love for yourself?
- Can you forgive yourself?
- What do you do to heal your spirit?
- Can you share your feelings with others?
- What are some of the most loving things that others have done for you?
- What are the loving things that you do for other people?
- Are you able to forgive others?
- What brings you joy and peace in your life?
- What can you do to feel alive and full of spirit?
- What traits do you like about yourself?
- What are your personal strengths?
- What life goals have you set for yourself?
- Do you ever feel at some level a connection with the world or universe?
- How does your environment have an impact on your state of well-being?
- What are your environmental stressors at work and at home?

- Do you incorporate strategies to reduce your environmental stressors?
- Are you concerned about the survival of the planet?
- Do you use relaxation or imagery skills?
- Do you meditate?
- Do you practice self-hypnosis?
- Do you believe in God or a higher power?
- Do you have a sense of belonging in this world?

Learning to trust one's inner knowing and to recognize its significance is an important component of spiritual growth. Moore's requirements of living artfully may be viewed as guides for being fully present, which is a crucial element of responding to needs of the spirit. The ability to listen deeply is also guided by these requirements of pausing, taking time, and being mindful Being with another, present in the particular moment and experience, involves a knowing that is of the intellect, heart, body, and spirit and may demand a deed that involves activity or being still and honoring the silence. [2]

The heart and soul of spirituality requires attention be paid to our Higher Self and significant connections. This process implies an ongoing practice of presence and intentional awareness that spirit is present in all relationships. As we become more intentional in our recognition of and response to the spirit present in each relationship, this spirit is reawakened.

AN EXERCISE IN SPIRITUAL AWAKENING

In chapters 6 and 7 I present several mind-body and self-hypnosis exercises to assist you in raising your self image and attain spiritual growth. Our thoughts have a way of blocking spirituality through self-criticism.

For example, when you view your body in a full-length mirror, do you say to yourself, "I don't like my body," "I'm too fat" or "I

wish my body was more or less so and so?" It is not so much that
we are, what we are as what we think.

If you think negative thoughts about your body, it starts becoming duller and loses vitality. If we think positive thoughts about
it, it starts becoming radiant and gains vitality. Our thoughts create our reality. Our body is just one more part of this reality. Begin
today the process of thinking of yourself as a thin, positive, ener-
getic and vibrant soul, and this will be the beginning of your new
reality. Tell your body how much you love and appreciate it when
you look in the mirror the first thing in the morning and it will
respond accordingly.

Try this simple exercise which consists merely of playing
relaxing, preferably New Age, music for about fifteen minutes.
Find a quiet place where you will be undisturbed and sit in a
comfortable chair or lie down on a recliner, couch or bed. I
highly recommend headphones to maximize the spiritual awak-
ening effect.

1. *Allow the relaxing and spiritual quality of this music to pulsate
   through your body. Feel your body entering into a peaceful altered
   state of consciousness.*
2. *Experience your body flowing and perhaps rising through space.
   You may perceive yourself floating on a cloud and being weightless.
   Even if you do leave your body there is no need for concern. You are
   perfectly safe.*
3. *Now see your body at your ideal weight and divinely beautiful. Feel
   your soul and its radiant inner beauty as it permeates throughout
   your physical body.*
4. *Visualize your physical body at its optimal well-being, physically, mentally, emotionally and spiritually. All the memory of this blissful state is
   now to be incorporated in the memory of each of your cells.*
5. *Begin to shape your body exactly as you desire it to be at your ideal
   weight and muscle tone. Picture yourself exactly as you want to look
   with the aid of your very soul to bring this image into your reality.*
6. *Take a few moments and add anything else to this ideal image*

of yourself. See yourself getting up and stepping into this new body. Your soul has made this possible, and is being purified as you make this transition.

In chapter 7 I will present exercises to train you to access your Higher Self (the perfect part of our soul—the "divine spark within us").

When you access your Higher Self and focus upon an ideal image of yourself, you not only will create a joyful, healthy and spiritual body, but you will also fulfill the larger purpose for which you were sent here to fulfill. That purpose is to create on the physical Earth, a perfect reflection of what you are as an eternal soul beyond Earth.

Always remind yourself of your spiritual potential and purpose as you practice the exercises in this book. As you tap into your soul and Higher Self, you will manifest the courage to commit yourself to positive choices and live them as fully as possible each day.

Most people make a change in their behavior when they are ready. No permanent change in eating habits, or anything else, results from coaxing, persuasive attempts or nagging by well-meaning friends and family. Changes occur in specific stages, often following setbacks and relapses. Raising your level of spirituality is the theme of this book to facilitate this goal and make it a permanent and natural part of your consciousness and awareness.

Do not be surprised when you experience a clarity about your very being that will create new beliefs that are rooted in a sensitive, loving understanding of yourself and others. This will help you make the kinds of breakthroughs that invite a full inflowing of health-giving forces into your emotions, your mind, and your body, and promote your ability to lose weight permanently and naturally.

CHAPTER 2

WHY DIETS DON'T WORK

You finally decide to commit yourself to lose weight. Perhaps a liquid diet drink is substituted for one or two meals. You might place yourself on the latest fad diet you read about in some book or magazine. The daily amount of calories you eat for several weeks is reduced to 1,000, or possibly 750 calories.

Soon you look great. A feeling of accomplishment exudes from your very being as you count up the pounds that you have lost Shortly thereafter your previous eating patterns surface. The pounds begin to return. Your weight eventually is higher than before you dieted.

This cycle is repeated. You lose weight, regain it, lose again and so on. Each time it appears that it takes longer to lose the weight and less time to put it back on. Will this yo-yo syndrome ever end?

Does this scenario sound familiar? Americans, about 60 percent who are overweight and approximately 35 percent who qualify as obese, turn to diets to lose weight. More than half of the nation is dieting or has dieted. But has this system of dieting worked?

Americans have been on thousands of diets during the past forty years. They obviously don't work permanently because they are only temporary measures. Temporary methods bring about temporary results. Permanent measures result in permanent changes.

Diets fail for many reasons. Most dieters focus on what they are going to eat when their ordeal is finally over. How can you possibly succeed on your diet when all you are thinking about is food? Depriving yourself is not the answer to healthy, permanent weight loss. It usually causes you to binge later on, which complicates the problem. Deprivation and bingeing become a vicious cycle, and that's just one of the many problems with dieting.

Another factor is the artificial regimentation involved in a diet. Many people who begin a diet are undisciplined. That is how they got into the overweight condition in the first place. Now they are expected to deprive themselves of their favorite foods and act like a marine recruit in boot camp. This is not a formula for success.

Each year the rate of obesity increases in America. Every decade or so higher weights are added to the recommended life insurance tables. If diets worked, the reverse trend should be apparent.

Still another confusion for the public is the contradicting theories represented by the diet sales pitches. One popular diet says to eat mostly protein and very few carbohydrates. Another equally popular diet says to eat mostly carbohydrates and very little protein. They both can't be right. Another plan says to eat whatever you feel like at the moment and then wash it out with pineapples and papayas. One more says to eat anything you can dream of, just weigh it first. And another says you should adhere to its program for only two weeks at a time. Yet another says to eat a small concoction of whatever you like, but be sure to exercise and be positive.

The most dangerous and ridiculous of these diets substitute "nutritional powders" for food. Most of these plans require tedious calorie counting and suggest daily weighings, both of which function only to frustrate the dieter and bring on feelings of guilt and depression.

Being overweight shortens both the quality and quantity of life. Nearly all long living peoples of the world, from Asia to South America to New Zealand, are lean. The greatest health, longevity and freedom from degenerative disease (heart disease, cancer, arthritis, etc.) are found among Americans who weigh fifteen percent under the recommended weights currently published.

There is one important universal truth to weight loss. That truth is that safe and permanent weight loss is directly related to the amount of vital energy (ATP) you have at your disposal, and to the efficient use of this energy to eliminate excess weight (as waste products) from your body.

The techniques presented throughout this book will fulfill this truth and work with your body to free up energy and reduce your weight until you reach an ideal weight that you can maintain for the rest of your life.

Dieting starves your body and forces it to pull energy from its own tissues. Instead of facilitating fat loss, this condition is interpreted by the body as a threat, and measures are instituted to conserve fat. What is burned for energy is muscle mass, and that is the worst possible scenario.

Muscle mass burns four to five times more calories than does fat. The longer you remain on a diet, the more muscle tissue you lose and the fewer muscle cells are left to burn calories. This is because fat cells are designed to hoard energy and see the body through long periods of hunger.

The result of this ill-fated mechanism is a slowing down of your metabolism in an attempt to conserve energy. This effect is even more dramatic if you don't exercise, since exercise builds up muscle tissue and this helps offset this slowdown in metabolism.

Another thing that occurs from dieting is weight loss, most of which is water. This results in burning fewer calories, since your body is left with proportionally less lean mass as well as less weight to carry and therefore continues to require fewer calories than it did to start with. If you resume eating "as usual," you will gain back on the number of calories that previously kept you stable. Simply eating high-fat foods (the most common pattern following a diet) with lower total calorie counts results in more of this fat ending up on your hips, waistline and thighs. This is due to the fact that more fat deposits are available with less lean muscle mass to burn incoming fat from food.

Weight cycling, or yo-yo dieting, results in frustration, discouragement and in no long term weight loss. Repeated episodes of this paradigm places you at higher risk for heart disease and other illness.

When you think about the time and energy that is spent in dieting, consider the following drains on your mind, body and time:

- Feeling weak and tired due to lack of food.
- Obsessing about food and not being able to accomplish personal or professional responsibilities.
- Feelings of guilt and frustration.
- Neurotic behavior, such as arguments with loved ones.
- Time wasted counting calories, weighing yourself and food, fantasizing about your favorite foods and so on.

The weight loss industry is a forty billion dollar enterprise. It uses television to sell its wares, among other media outlets. Ironically, television itself is one device that has contributed more to weight problems than anything I can think of.

Studies have shown that approximately twenty percent of people who watch more than three hours of television a week are overweight, compared to just 4.5 percent of those who watch less than an hour. The prevalence of obesity in adolescents increased by 2 percent for every additional hour of television watched per day. The average American teenager today watches up to forty hours of television per week, compared with just eighteen hours in 1968. At this rate, each new generation will be about 6 percent fatter than the last.

There are four ways in which watching television adds to an individual's weight problem:

1. It prevents you from being physically active and burning up calories. Since you hardly have to move, your metabolism drops to its minimal resting rate.
2. Television ads promote high-fat foods. You are brainwashed into eating the worst possible foods for your health and weight.
3. You are programmed to rush into the kitchen immediately and grab something to eat. This speeds up your eating habits.

4. These television ads also promote the ingestion of more foods than you need. The "super sizing" advocated by fast food chains are a classic example.

OTHER REASONS FOR FAILIURES IN DIETING

Most individuals will lose weight if they set their daily caloric intake below 1,500. Many moderately obese patients can't tolerate this diet long enough to reach their ideal weight. Even relatively "sound" diet programs give slow and sometimes frustrating results—about a half pound per week. The majority of patients who endure the program long enough to reach their goal regain everything lost within a year or two. Most of these are rigid and boring. As I previously stated, several are hazardous to your health.

Conflicting cultural messages are presented to us by the desire to maintain healthy eating habits, yet still maintain a proper weight. For instance, on one hand society programs us to think?

*   Being overweight is "bad."
*   Being thin makes you a better person.
*   You can never be too rich or too thin.
*   Only thin people are truly successful.
*   Thin people don't have to work at it.
*   Thin people get to eat satisfying food.

We are at the same time fed (no pun intended) the following messages:

*   You can't have fun without food.
*   Food is a reward and means of celebration.
*   Food is more fun than exercise!
*   Food helps numb bad feelings, such as shame.
*   Fatty food tastes better than lean food.
*   Food is for comfort and escape.

DYSFUNCTIONAL EATING BEHAVIORS

Because of negative programming by society, environmental circumstances and numerous other factors, four major forms of dysfunctional eating behaviors are exhibited. These are compulsive eating, emotional eating, the overeater and the non-exerciser.

THE COMPULSIVE EATER

The critical factor for the compulsive eater is control. They simply cannot prevent themselves from bingeing occasionally. Overly strict rules are adopted to maintain a certain weight. Since it is practically impossible to live this type of ascetic lifestyle, a bingeing outlet is their solution.

The more severe the controls and limitations we place on ourselves, the more likely we are to violate them. Certain healthy solutions to this pattern are to exercise moderately and regularly, learn how to lose weight sensibly and gradually, learn how to eat rather than diet, develop other avenues of interest and become more open to the concept of error.

THE EMOTIONAL EATER

When people are brought up in an environment in which food was utilized to eliminate negative feelings, emotional eating is often the result. This also applies to the association of food with reward.

Health mechanisms to eliminate this pattern are the use of exercise to deal with stress, cultivating nonfood sources of relaxation and comfort and keeping low-fat foods handy.

THE OVEREATER

People who impulsively eat whenever they want and whatever they please tend to be overeaters. Most commonly, they were raised on high-fat foods such as hamburgers, steak, milk shakes, potato chips and so on.

This individual eats robotically, without realizing how much or exactly what they consumed. Neither compulsive nor emotional factors characterize this style of eating. Successful methods to eliminate this pattern are to use low-fat alternatives, monitor food choices and consumption patterns until eating becomes a completely conscious process and adopting a regular exercise regimen as diversion.

THE NONEXERCISER

Busy working people tend to run out of time to do regular exercise. They look upon exercise as a boring chore that takes up valuable time.

A simple solution to this pattern is to enhance the activities of daily life so they require more energy expenditure on a regular basis. For example, you might park at the far end of a parking lot requiring you to walk more to reach your office. Using stairs in place of the elevator, speed-walking at lunch instead of sitting in a restaurant and stretching every thirty minutes are other examples.

FASTING

The problem with fasting is two-fold. First, the body is denied essential nutrients, and secondly most fasters return to their old eating habits and end up gaining weight.

Other problems noted with fasting are:

- A deficiency in calcium, magnesium, potassium, and phosphorous, with consequent deterioration of bones (not always immediately detectable) and teeth.

- Lowered sex drive in men and women and an increase in menstrual problems in women.
- Increase frequency of gout, stomach ulcers and adrenal exhaustion.
- A tendency towards bingeing.

BINGE EATING

High levels of a brain chemical called neuropeptide Y and low levels of the neurotransmitter serotonin are found in the morning following a fast. These chemicals trigger a strong desire for carbohydrates. This explains the popularity of pancakes, fruit, waffles and toast with jelly. This urge becomes stronger the longer the fast continues.

Another chemical produced by the brain is galanin. This substance triggers a desire for fatty foods and is involved in the conversion of dietary fat into body fat. Galanin levels rise throughout the day, even following the ingestion of fatty foods!

Galanin levels soar when we fast and our body is forced to burn its own fat to supply energy. This effect, along with the neuropeptide Y and serotonin I mentioned earlier, causes a craving for high-fat and carbohydrate foods. Bingeing is the result.

Bingeing Eating Disorder (BED) involves eating large quantities of food in a short period of time with a feeling of loss of control. It affects about one-third of overweight individuals, especially women, and millions more "normal-weight" women who appear to have balanced eating patterns. The triggers for binge eating are different for men and women. Women tend to eat more when they are angry, sad or depressed. Men are more likely to binge when they are feeling happy or socializing with others.

EFFECTIVE WEIGHT LOSS

The most effective and reasonable way to lose weight is to reduce fat intake while increasing physical activity to a moderate level. This is not to imply a rapid or dramatic loss of weight. An effective weight loss is any weight loss that results from healthful, reasonable, and permanent changes in eating habits and physical activity. This weight loss is sustainable throughout adult life.

Regardless of your history with dieting, your resting metabolism, distribution of body fat, and prospects for future permanent weight loss are unaffected by past dieting. Even if you have been a yo-yo dieter for years, you needn't worry that you've ruined your metabolism. What is required now is an alteration in your definition of "normal" living to mean, lean, and active living for the rest of your life.

From the thousands of patients I have worked with since 1974 in training them to lose weight, I have found that their ideal weight is not determined by charts, envy, or wishful thinking. It is the natural result of a healthy lifestyle and improved self-image.

I have worked with patients desiring to lose anywhere from five to one hundred and twenty-five pounds. The solution to their goals are always the same—adopt the lifestyle that is specified in the definition of effective weight loss.

You do not need to diet "better" in the short term but to quit dieting and calorie counting. Unwanted pounds are the result of too little exercise and too much fat, not too much of nutritional food. The lower the percentage of fat in our diet (and the higher the percentage of carbohydrates) the lower our percentage of body fat.

Consider for a moment the fact that only three percent of the total calories in a pat of butter are burned off during its passage from your mouth, through the digestive tract, to your thigh or midriff. Now factor in the efficiency of carbohydrates in providing immediate energy. Twenty-three percent of the calories in a fat-free bagel are burned off during digestion. Eating carbohydrates instead of fat results in a twenty percent calorie discount.

Most of us will become healthier and leaner if we reduce our typical forty percent fat diet to twenty percent. A recent survey of more than 18,000 Americans revealed that people who regularly walk, jog, cycle, or do aerobics weigh less than people who do not exercise, regardless of calorie intake, height, race, smoking status, or education. [3]

The difference between dieting alone and exercising coupled with proper nutrition can be summed up as follows: dieting alone burns lean muscle tissue, while exercising builds and preserves lean muscle tissue, which in turn will burn more calories, making it harder for you to regain the lost fat.

CHAPTER 3

HOW WE GAIN AND LOSE WEIGHT

CALORIES AND METABOLISM

In order to understand how the body gains and loses weight, a discussion of calories and metabolism is necessary. Metabolism refers to the process by which the food and oxygen that we consume are transported by the blood to our tissues where they are used for energy, bone care, growth and tissue repair.

Metabolism is a measure of energy in the form of calories, heat, food or exercise. A calorie is a unit of heat. The heat necessary to raise the temperature of one pint of water eight degrees Fahrenheit is equal to one calorie.

One important principle of physiology you should know is that 3500 calories equals one pound. If we take into the body 3500 calories more than are needed to meet our energy needs, we have gained one pound of excess fat. By taking in 3500 calories less than our body requires (or burning up this same amount in excess of our consumption of food), we will lose exactly one pound of fat. It doesn't matter how long it requires to accomplish this feat.

Overweight people retain no more calories from their food that does anyone else. Obesity is not due to metabolism problems. Gland disorders are not the reason people are overweight. Overeating is the cause of weight problems.

Energy, as well as heat, is represented by basal metabolism. This is based on calories while the individual relaxes, fasts and rests in a room of normal temperature. Basal metabolism is thus the lowest number of calories necessary for the maintenance of bodily functions with ease as to physical, mental and digestive comfort and safety.

Our metabolism increases as we move around at work or play. Emotions also affect our metabolic rate. A slower rise in metabolism is noted following the ingestion of fats and carbohydrates, as compared to proteins. Calorie expenditure is increased more by exercise than in any other way. Strenuous exercise may result in an increase in our basal metabolism by a factor of as much as ten to fifteen times over our resting rate!

If you are overweight it is because you eat more calories than your body requires. You are putting more fuel into your body than it can utilize. The excess fuel or energy is stored as fat. Someone else, with quite different nutritional needs, might very well lose weight on the same amount of food.

Walking thirty-six miles would result in the loss of a pound. A 300-pound man would only need to eat one slice of bread to replace the energy utilized in walking up fifteen flights of steps. To put it simply, 3,500 calories equals one pound of fat.

Most people gain weight as they age, especially around middle age. Today researchers attribute this drop in metabolism to a drop in physical activity, with its associated decrease in lean muscle mass. This results in a loss of calorie-burning lean mass tissue, which in turn causes them to gain more easily even if they eat the same or less food.

Keeping physically active throughout life will function to reverse this trend. The fitter we are at any age, the less we will have to worry about our weight. This is because we will produce and maintain an ample supply of lean muscle tissue, which burns calories at a much higher rate than fat tissue.

Temporary weight gain is explained by simple biology. We gain about two pounds each day as water weight, which is gone by the following morning. On a day when we consume a great quantity of food and drink we may gain up to five pounds of temporary weight. This temporary weight gain is not a problem, unless you allow it to upset you emotionally. This fluid loss also explains why more weight is lost in the first week of dieting than in the same length of time thereafter.

Weight fluctuation of a temporary nature can be due to illness. Fevers burn extra calories and colds often are associated with a lowered appetite. These minor gains or losses end when you resume your normal lifestyle.

Injuries, especially chronic ones, can exert a greater effect on weight. When we are in pain a cessation of activity is often the behavior we adopt. This is often accompanied by an increase in our eating out of boredom or frustration.

A better solution is to engage in some minor activity that not only will help keep weight down and muscle tone up, but will actually aid in healing the injury. For example, if you sprained your ankle and can no longer jog, consider swimming, weight training or activities that only involve your arms to burn up calories and keep the muscles toned.

What may very well be a warning sign that something is wrong with our body is a sudden weight gain beyond the fluid retention I previously described. If you respond to this gain by initiating a starvation diet or obsessively counting calories, you will most probably take energy and attention away from the more central tasks of identifying and changing the circumstances that prompted the weight gain in the first place.

For the sake of health, people who are twenty percent or more above their ideal weight should reduce. But frequent dieters have a higher death rate and as much as a 50 percent higher risk of heart disease than people with stable weight who do not diet. Any large sudden weight change, either down or up (pregnancy excluded), seems to increase the risk of death due to heart disease.

Stabilizing our weight, rather than continually straining to lose this unwanted poundage over and over again is far healthier. The more slowly you lose, however, the more likely you are to keep the weight off. For the sake of your health as well as to safeguard against regain, you should never lose more than two to four pounds per month.

Quick fixes never work in the long run. Whenever I have assisted an obese person to reach their ideal weight and maintain it for at least two years, most of their psychological problems cease to exist. This leads me to conclude that the psychological problems of many overweight people are more often the result and not the cause of their overeating.

The most important factor is not how much you weigh, but how much of your daily diet and your weight consists of fat. It also matters how that fat is distributed in your body. If most of your fat is centered around your middle, then your body type is what researchers call an "apple" type. If your largest fat deposits are located in your lower body, namely the hips, thighs, and buttocks, then your body type is considered a "pear" type. Most men are apples, most women pears.

WEIGHT AND ENERGY EXPENDITURE

The two most important factors that determine your caloric needs are your current weight and the energy you expend. A more active person uses up more energy, and subsequently requires more calories to maintain their current weight. The main reason dieting won't work is it goes against our basic requirements for calories.

For example, a 140 pound woman requires 1,250 calories, if she is inactive, to maintain her weight. If she is only a little active this figure rises to 1,630 calories. 1,750 calories are necessary for a moderately active 140 pound woman, and 1,880 calories for a highly active woman to maintain this weight. The general rule of thumb for determining the amount of calories required to maintain your weight is for a woman to multiply her weight by 11, 12 for a man. [4]

Eating properly will result in a lean figure. Calories are our fuel. If we reduce this fuel consumption improperly by dieting, we convert our high energy burning lean muscle mass to energy: a poor solution.

Eating beyond our calorie requirements causes the production and storage of fat: one pound for every 3,500 unused calories.

From this discussion we can see that calories are our friend. Here is a breakdown of the calories from the three types of food:

1 gram of protein	=	4 calories
1 gram of carbohydrates	=	4 calories
1 gram of fat	=	9 calories

We can eat twice as much of protein and carbohydrates as compared to fats and still not ingest the same amount of calories! An intelligent approach to nutrition is simply to cut back on fats and eat more carbohydrates and protein.

This means that we can increase the bulk or amount of certain foods, eat often throughout the day and provide our body with its calorie requirements, while losing weight during this process. I will discuss selecting proper foods and eating to reach and maintain your ideal weight in the next chapter.

For the cells of the body to receive and use vital nutrients, ingested food must be changed into simpler chemicals. These simpler substances are the products of digestion, a series of mechanical and chemical processes that take place in the digestive tract. Carbohydrates are converted into glucose, while fats become broken down into fatty acids and proteins into amino acids. Through a rather complicated mechanism known as the Krebs cycle, all of these basic substances are transformed into energy in the form of ATP for use by our body.

Discoveries by the early 1950s had given rise to a "dual-center theory" of control of eating. According to this theory the hypothalamus of the brain contains the primary control centers for hunger and satiety: A "hunger center" in the lateral hypothalamus (LH) facilities eating, whereas a "satiety center" in the ventromedial hypothalamus (VMH) inhibits eating. All the other regions and factors that influence eating were presumed to act through these hypothalamic control centers.

The body monitors its food stores. An indication that these supplies are falling below a set value could be the trigger that activates the feeding system. Many different indices of food stocks have been suggested. Among most prominent are the rate of utilization of glucose and the supply of fat, which may be indicated by some by-product, such as free fatty acids.

Glucose, especially in the presence of insulin, stimulates the VMH (a part of the satiety system) and inhibits the LH (a part of the feeding system). On the other hand, free fatty acids stimulate the LH and inhibit the VMH; their presence in the blood may indicate that fat stores are being drawn upon. Thus initiation of the disposition to eat could be signaled by lack of glucose or by presence of free fatty acids or both. It is not the absolute level of glucose but rather than rate of glucose utilization that is monitored by cells in the hypothalamus. We usually report feeling hungry at mealtimes, even if they have eaten only a few hours previously and are in no significant state of depletion. Is this just habit or "imagination?" The release of insulin has been observed when experimental subjects look at food at mealtime or when they imagine food intake as a result of hypnotic suggestion.

In primitive times our species faced a scarcity of food and a great need to exert ourselves to provide nourishment for ourselves and our family. Today things are quite different. We now have an abundance of rich, palatable food and very little need for exertion and exercise of any type.

Overweight people are hypothesized to be more responsive to external stimuli of all sorts than are their peers of average weight; they are also hypothesized to be less responsive to internal physiological cues that affect eating. The heightened susceptibility of obese individuals to external cues is evident in their spontaneous pattern of eating. For example, obese people, being more responsive to food, eat longer meals, but they also tend to eat fewer meals, presumably because when food is not present, they exert less effort to obtain it. Most people, and not just the obese, are strongly influenced by external dietary stimuli and are poor at judging internal cues to nutritional need or satiety.

SET POINTS

Although adults differ greatly in their body weights, at any stage
of life each person tends to keep his or her body weight quite
constant. For this reason some investigators state that each person
"defends" a *set point* or target value of body weight. People whose
body weight had been reduced an average of 25% through a semi-
starvation diet in an experiment, rapidly regained their
predeprivation weight when allowed to eat as they pleased. Dieting makes people more responsive to food. People whose set point
for weight is high and who are trying to restrain their intake are
the ones who are especially stimulated by the presence of food.

HOW TO DETERMINE IF YOU ARE
OVERWEIGHT

The build or size of an individual should never be used as the sole
criterion for proper weight. People come in all shapes and sizes,
and what is normal weight for one person is not necessarily proper
for another. The important thing to note is that the build and size
should be compatible.

Forty percent of the weight of our body is from muscle tissue.
When food is transported to a tissue it produces more of the same
kind of tissue. The more muscles we use, the more muscle weight
we will possess and the stronger we will be. The reverse is also true.

Thirty percent of our weight should be fat. As we will discuss
in chapter 4, it should be monosaturated fat. Fat is necessary to
supply energy to cells, organs and tissues. Almost all subcutane-
ous parts of our body contain storage bins for fat.

Although exercise improves the texture and strength of muscles,
it cannot replace the necessity of food. Food is required for building
muscles and for supplying energy to our body. When overeating results in the storage of excessive fat, exercise alone cannot dissolve it.
We always need a proper balance between diet and exercise.

Here are three tests to determine if you contain too much fat:

1. *Lie on your back and place a ruler from your ribs, where they flare, to your pubic region. Being at your proper weight will be indicated by the ruler lying flat. If one end is raised higher then you have too much fat on your body.*
2. *Pinch your skin under the rib farthest down from your armpit. If you have less than one half inch you are too thin. Over one inch of fat here indicates you are overweight.*
3. *The distance around the chest, at the level of the nipples, should be greater by a few inches than the distance around the abdomen on a level with the navel if you are at a proper weight.*

CARBOHYDRATE ADDICTION

Although carbohydrates are an excellent source of energy and contain less than half the calories of fat, addiction to this food group is a serious problem that affects weight gain.

As many as 75 percent of overweight people, and 40 percent of normal-weight people, suffer from a biological imbalance involving insulin. Insulin assists our body to use and conserve food energy by ordering the body to store energy as fat when no food is available, delivering food energy to the tissues that require it and directing your body when to eat.

This hormone may easily be overproduced by the pancreas and this imbalance leads to a cycle in which we experience overpowering cravings for carbohydrates, such as breads, pastas, snack foods and cakes. To further aggravate this situation, the ingestion of these carbohydrates stimulates the pancreas to release even more insulin.

Constant hunger pangs intense and recurrent cravings for carbohydrates, easy weight gain and difficulty in losing weight results. Weaning yourself off excessive amounts of carbohydrates will often correct this hormonal imbalance so that you can lose weight and be healthy for the rest of your life, without feeling deprived or struggling to manage your eating patterns and your weight.

Consider the following six questions:

1. Do you get tired after eating a large meal or find that you get sluggish and/or hungry in the afternoon?
2. Do you find it harder to take off weight, and keep it off, than when you were younger?
3. Does stress, boredom or tiredness make you want to eat?
4. After eating a full breakfast, do you get hungrier before it is time for lunch than you would if you had skipped breakfast altogether?
5. Do you sometimes feel that you aren't satisfied, even though you have just finished a meal?
6. Have you been on diet after diet, only to regain all the weight that you lost and more?

A "yes" response to two of these questions suggests a mild addiction to carbohydrates. Three or four affirmative responses indicates a moderate addiction, whereas a severe addiction is suggested by five or six "yes" answers.[5]

ALLERGIES

Some people are attracted to the very foods they are allergic to. Such a food (allergen) produces a "hang over" effect several hours after it is eaten. These symptoms include:

- Fatigue
- Headache
- Depression
- Nervousness
- Light-headedness
- Uncontrolled craving for more of this food.

For example, wheat, chocolate, eggs, and milk are some of the most common documented allergens for causing migraine headaches. Work-environment pollutants, toilet bowl cleaners, insecticides and bathroom deodorizers have been known to trigger binge eating. Eliminating these allergens will often result in the removal of both the headaches and bingeing, and subsequently result in a loss of weight.

GLANDULAR PROBLEMS

As I stated earlier, most weight gain or loss is due to our eating habits. The thyroid gland, located in the throat on each side of the windpipe, contains the hormone thyroxin. Thyroxin greatly effects our metabolism. A depletion of this hormone causes an increase in weight and vice versa.

There are ways to determine if your production of thyroxin is too low (hypothyroidism). Medical tests easily reveal this situation. The most common symptoms of hypothyroidism are:

1. Lethargy.
2. Dry, coarse skin.
3. Swelling eyelids.
4. Fatigue.
5. Feeling cold, particularly in the hands and feet.
6. Weight gain or inability to lose weight, despite constant attempts at dieting.
7. Loss of sexual desire and enjoyment of sex (low libido).
8. Impotence.
9. Heart palpitation.
10. Emotional instability.
11. Brittle nails.
12. Muscle weakness, pain.
13. Pain in joints.
14. Poor concentration and memory.
15. Anemia.
16. Atherosclerosis.
17. High cholesterol levels.
18. Labored, difficult breathing.
19. Swelling feet.

20. Hoarseness.
21. Nervousness.
22. Depression.
23. Coarse hair.
24. Pale skin.
25. Enlarged heart.
26. Faulty memory.
27. Constipation.
28. Hair loss.

The occurrence of two or more of the first five symptoms and/or six or more of the remaining twenty-three is highly indicative of hypothyroidism. My recommendation is to see an endocrinologist and have the appropriate tests conducted.

You can resolve a thyroid problem by simply adding more iodine-containing foods to your diet. Good sources of iodine are:

• Shrimp
• Crab
• Lobster
• Haddock
• Cod
• Herring
• Halibut
• Kelp
• Cod liver oil

Even if you do have hypothyroidism, this does not cause weight problems. Hypothyroidism simply slows down the body's rate of metabolism. If you reduced the amount of calories eaten, you will still lose weight. It may take longer to register this weight loss, but it will occur nevertheless.

CHAPTER 4

EATING TO REACH AND MAINTAIN YOUR

IDEAL WEIGHT

While I do not advocate any diet per se, I most certainly recommend you read the labels of foods before you purchase them. Investigate before you consume is the catch phrase here.

Many typical American diets incorporate between 37 and 43 percent as fat—that is too high. I suggest you do not exceed 30 percent, nor consume below 15 percent of fat—remember, our body is 15 percent by weight fat.

Consider this label of food contents per serving of a certain type of food product:

Calories	36 calories
Protein	1 gram
Carbohydrates	4 grams
Fat	2 grams

To determine the fat content multiply the number of grams by 9, since each gram of fat contains 9 calories.

$$2 \times 9 = 18$$

Now divide the number of fat calories by the total calories.

$$18/36 = 50 \text{ percent}$$

This hypothetical food product is 50 percent fat—far too high for a proper diet. Whether this product was advertised as "low-fat" "one-third less calories" or whatever, it is unacceptable for your goal of reaching and maintaining your ideal weight.

Here is another example of a "light" potato chip label:

Calories	130
Protein	2 grams
Carbohydrate	19 grams
Fat	6 grams
Sodium	140 mg

Using our formula we see that the fat content is 42 percent

$6 \times 9 = 54$

$54/130 = 42$ percent

130 total calories

I hardly consider 42 percent light. Let the buyer beware of the evil lurking in the mind and sound bites of Madison Avenue.

Another example of improper use of the term light is represented by a well-known Philadelphia cream cheese label that promotes itself as "light."

Serving size	1 oz.
Calories	60
Protein	3 grams
Carbohydrates	2 grams
Fat	5 grams

$5 \times 9 = 45$

$45/60 = 75$ percent

Now we have a new definition of "light." This suggests that 75 percent fat content is actually good for you—it isn't. Do not depend on adjectives and sales pitches for your nutrition. A simple calculation will determine what is nutritious versus what is fattening. If you don't like carrying pencils and paper with you to the supermarket, simply bring a small calculator. It is well worth the effort.

In the beginning I advocate purchasing a nutrition book that details the amounts of fats in every food you are likely to eat. Simply write down everything that you consume and total the number of grams and fats. Now compute the total calories eaten that same day and figure out your fat percentage.

By simply multiplying the number of fat grams by 9 and dividing this figure by the total daily calories, you arrive at the average percentage of fat for that day.

After a short while of doing this, you will develop a feel for the kind and amount of foods that will keep your fat percentage between say 20 to 30 percent. This recommendation of less than thirty percent fat content is shared by such authorities as Nathan Pritikin, Georgia Kostas, Dean Ornish, Scott Grundy, Gail Butterfield and John McDougal.

Do not be concerned if occasionally your fat content exceeds 30 percent. Even a day during which you exceed 50 percent will be more than balanced out by all of the days you kept your fat percentage below 30 percent. You will still be losing weight permanently and naturally.

When I was growing up peanut butter and jelly sandwiches were a staple. Which is better for our ideal weight goal, the jam or the peanut butter?

For my example I will use Smucker's seedless red raspberry jam and Jif creamy peanut butter:

JAM
Serving size	1 Tbsp (20g)
Calories	50
Total fat	0 g
Sodium	0 mg
Total Carb.	13 g
Sugars	12 g
Protein	0 g

Fat percentage	0
PEANUT BUTTER	
Serving size	2 Tbsp (32g)
Calories	190
Total fat	130 grams
Fat percentage	68.4

It is easy to see that today I have more jam on bagel breakfasts than peanut butter and jam lunches. Investigate before you consume.

Always remember that not all calories are created equal. It is far more desirable to obtain our calories from carbohydrates than from fat. Protein sources do stress our kidney, especially in the form of red meat. We need all three food sources, it is just a matter of ratios.

As you shall see later in this chapter, following my recommendations will allow you to eat whatever you want, whenever you desire and however much of it you want. By properly programming your subconscious (see chapters 6 and 7), along with healthier food choices, you can follow this pattern and still lose weight permanently and naturally.

Adopting a low-fat, high-volume eating paradigm will free you from pills, powders, instant shakes and rabbit food. The result will quite simply be a healthier, leaner and stronger you.

Here are simple rules to follow to change your life and feel better physically, mentally, emotionally and spiritually:

1. Never fear food again. Food is our friend. We need it to survive and thrive. Just alter your past eating patterns and you will be home free.
2. Eat as much as you want. Even when you don't feel like eating, make sure that your body is receiving at the minimum what your weight and activity level require for energy. Read labels and keep your fat percentage below 30 percent.

3. Never skip a meal again. I have already described the dangers of starvation to our body. The fact that this mechanism results in weight gain and obsessive behavior should be enough to convince you to eliminate this panic method of losing weight.

Eat when you are hungry. The times of your meals may vary, but make sure you eat when your body sends you physiologic signals—hunger pangs. A breakfast consisting of fruit, coffee, juice, bagels and cereal is quite a lot of food, but low in fat and high in volume. This is going to assist you in losing weight forever.

Keep your meals to at least three per day and build from there. By eliminating the sugary cereal or pancake with loads of syrup and butter breakfasts, the cheeseburger with French fries lunch and the steak, potato and milk dinners (not counting snacks), you are well on your way to your ideal weight.

Here are my recommendations for the various food groups:

Fruit

If you were trapped on an island and could only select one food group to live on for several months, the best choice would be fruit. The fructose, or sugar, from fruit burns quickly, but is not that filling.

Another innovation is dried fruits. They are packed with soluble fiber, the type that dissolves in water. Foods high in soluble fiber keep you full, strong and do not result in extra weight. These fiber-rich foods keep your insulin and blood sugar levels low following a meal.

Fiber-rich foods slow your rate of absorption of fat and results in less new fat produced by the liver. You will find these foods tasty and ideal for mid-morning or mid-afternoon snacks. Examples of dried fruits with soluble fiber are peaches, prunes, apricots and figs.

Vegetables

The second best food for your trapped on an island scenario are vegetables. You will find that vegetables alone will not satisfy your hunger, no matter how many celery sticks or plain salads you eat. Include this food group with pasta salads, on your sandwich, with rice salads and as a side dish.

For high-soluble-fiber vegetables try turnips, brussel sprouts, cabbage, okra and parsnips. You would be surprised how popular these foods are becoming with gourmet delis.

Whole Grains

These foods are a great source of complex carbohydrates. Rice, for example, can be prepared in numerous different ways. My prerequisites of low-fat, high-volume and high-quality food are more than satisfied by whole grains.

Breakfast cereal not only makes an excellent way to start your day, but a healthy snack too. The following cereals have the greatest percentage of soluble fiber:

- Uncooked oat grain
- Heartwise K
- All Bran
- Oat Bran Crunch

Lean Protein

Most of us were raised on red meat as our major source of protein. There is no such thing as lean beef. By composition beef is low-volume, high-fat and a saturated-fat food. Pork is also a high-fat source of protein.

We will deal with beans, or legumes shortly. Fish (except bluefish, mackerel and salmon), lean egg white, white turkey, and white chicken are lean options for protein food.

Legumes

Beans will fulfill your protein requirements without the saturated fat. Combining legumes with vegetables and grains most definitely satisfy all of your protein needs.

One of the best hunger-killing foods are beans. These high in soluble fiber, filling, tasty and powerfully energizing foods are inexpensive and readily available. Uncooked beans are better than cooked ones.

Kidney beans, soybeans, butter beans and pinto beans are among your choices. The possibility of gas following bean consumption can be easily handled by the following recommendations:

- Soak the beans overnight before eating them.
- Chew beans slowly and take small bites.
- Lentils, garbanzos and pinto beans promote the least gas. Keep away from white beans.
- Eat small amounts of beans more frequently instead of a few large meals.

PROCESSED GRAINS AND STARCHES

We tend to obtain most of our carbohydrates from processed carbohydrates, such as white bread. Processed grains and starches include pasta, cornmeal, bagels, instant rice and whole wheat. These foods are low-fat and high-volume, but are not high quality foods. Much of the fiber and nutritional value are lost during the manufacturing process. Still, these are far better than doughnuts and pastries for breakfast or lunch.

When you go to the supermarket read labels and plan your shopping list. It is much easier to say "no" in the supermarket than it is at home after you have purchased high-fat foods that you feel obligated to "use up." Furthermore, any wrinkles and looseness of skin firm up with time after significant weight loss.

WHAT YOU SHOULD BE EATING

CARBOHYDRATES

Complex carbohydrates should be on the top of your shopping list. Foods that comprise this group are potatoes, bread, pasta, grains, cereals, bagels, rice and low-fat crackers. Approximately half of the calories we consume should come from this group.

Carbohydrates are the first to burn as fuel and the last to be stored as fat. They contain chemicals, such as serotonin, that trigger the brain to lift our mood and reduce our appetite.

By eating carbohydrates without an accompanying high-fat food, you encourage your body to burn its existing fat. Since our brain uses only calories derived from carbohydrates and requires a minimum of 400 calories each day to function, this further emphasizes the importance of this food group.

Sugar is no more fattening than any other kind of carbohydrate or than protein, since it contains 4 calories per gram. This is less than half the calories of fat. There is nothing wrong with a little sugar in our coffee or tea. Sugar promotes leanness by lowering your appetite for high-fat treats.

The problem with sugar is that it contains no nutritional components, and is not very filling. One Tootsie Roll Pop has the same amount of calories as three peaches!

When sugar is eaten together with fat, the combination may be especially likely to wind up around your waist or hips. Sugar stimulates the release of insulin, which in turn encourages fat to be stored. Foods such as chocolate bars, doughnuts, pie, and full-fat ice cream may be more fattening than their calories and fat count suggest. They are more fattening than nonfat sweets such as frozen yogurt, jelly beans, gumdrops, or licorice.

Fibers represent complex carbohydrates that resist breakdown by our digestive tract. Vegetables, whole grains and fruits are examples of this class of foods. Some advantages of high-fiber foods are:

- A reduction in blood cholesterol levels from water-soluble fibers in legumes, oats, carrots and fruit.
- Reduction in intestinal cancer by the insoluble fiber present in whole grains and beans. Make sure the product contains between four and five grams of bran per one-ounce serving.
- An easy bowel movement by making stool softer and easier to pass through the colon.

- Better control over the levels of blood sugar and insulin from the fibers in legumes and fruit.
- People who regularly eat high-fiber foods tend to weigh less and have less body fat than people with low-fiber eating habits.
- High-fiber foods contains a built-in calorie deduction because the calories contained in the fiber are included in the food's official calorie count but are not usable by the body.

Men should eat 50 grams of fiber daily, whereas women need about 40 grams. This represents about twice as much as most people consume. Drink plenty of fluids with your fiber meals and don't limit yourself to one type of fiber.

PROTEIN

Protein is neither an appetite suppressant nor a metabolic boon. Although it is an essential nutrient, most of us eat at least twice as much protein as our bodies really require for good health. An adult (neither pregnant nor nursing) requires about .36 grams of protein per pound of ideal body weight. A 152 pound person needs 54.72 grams of protein daily.

This can be obtained from merely one double cheeseburger. You pay the price for this with the high fat content of beef. The richest sources of vegetable protein are soybeans, black beans, chickpeas and brown beans. These foods are nearly fat free, contain plenty of fiber and are quite filling.

Unlike carbohydrates, excess protein must go through the kidneys, where the nitrogen in the protein molecule is removed for excretion before the rest of the protein can be changed into usable calories or fat. An excessive protein intake places an unnecessary and potentially dangerous burden on the kidneys. Too much protein can also create a deficit in calcium, which will cause a weakening of bones and teeth.

We lose fat by eating plenty of carbohydrates with just enough protein as our body needs for good health. Low-fat, high-volume and high-quality foods are our goal.

HERE ARE SOME ADDITIONAL HELPFUL HINTS TO EATING RIGHT

- Sip on no-calorie beverages throughout meal.
- Don't eat your meals while doing other distracting things like watching TV or reading.
- Cook soups and stews a day earlier than needed, so you can skim off congealed fat before reheating.
- Put away leftovers or extra servings as soon as food is served.
- Use plain, low-, or non-fat yogurt in place of sour cream on baked potatoes.
- Eat slowly; pace yourself; take small bites, and chew well.
- Eat nuts more often than nut butters.
- Serve from kitchen, i.e., don't put food platters on table.
- Include soup in many or most meals. Research has shown that people who routinely begin meals with a bowl of soup tend to be pounds lighter than people who rarely have soup. Make sure that the soups on your menu are vegetable or broth based rather than cream based.
- Remove visible fat from meat and poultry.
- Brown food in nonstick pans to eliminate cooking fats.
- Use nonstick spray coating, preferably containing lecithin, instead of greasing or buttering baking pans or casseroles.
- Eat on a smaller plate so that amount of food appears larger.
- Remove skin from poultry before baking or roasting.
- In restaurants:
  A. Avoid all-you-can-eat or buffets whenever possible—order from the menu.
  B. Have the waiter remove your plate promptly when you have had your fill and order a hot beverage to sip on.
  C. Ask for a doggie bag.
- When attending parties:
  A. Don't go overly hungry; eat a little something before you go.
  B. Survey the selections before choosing.

   C. Take low-fat alternatives.
- Cook with wine to prepare tasty meals that are devoid of salts and fat. Nearly all of the alcohol and calories are burned off during cooking, but the enriching flavor remains. Avoid wines labeled as cooking wines, as they contain too much salt. Use olive oil instead of margarine or polyunsaturated cooking oils.
- Don'ts to be immediately incorporated in your life:
  A. Don't forget that your most valuable qualities have nothing to do with the size or shape of your body.
  B. Don't diet.
  C. Don't weigh yourself.
  D. Don't count calories.
  E. Don't allow food, weight, and body image to consume your thoughts.

ELIMINATING BINGEING FOREVER

Here is why a low-fat, high-carbohydrate, high-activity, eat-when-you're hungry lifestyle will eliminate your urge to binge:

- Exercise reduces stress and keeps a proper balance of brain chemicals that minimize the desire to binge on high-fat foods.
- High-carbohydrate and low-fat diets reduce the level of galanin in our blood.
- The levels of neuropeptide Y and serotonin are also now kept, in proper balance, preventing cravings for additional carbohydrates.
- By substituting low-fat treats (such as chocolate frozen yogurt) for high-fat snacks (such as chocolate ice cream) we are not depriving our body of the class of food, just changing the quality. This eliminates the need to binge.

- The feelings of anguish and desperation so common with diets are eliminated, since you are eating foods you enjoy and whenever you feel hungry.

OTHER NUTRIENTS OUR BODY NEEDS AND HOW TO SUPPLY THEM

TRYPTOPHAN

One essential amino acid that is required to produce serotonin and that is not produced by our body is tryptophan. This amino acid encourages sound sleep. By sleeping better we can avoid those midnight snacks.

Serotonin is produced from glucose, so it is not unusual to find overweight people attracted to refined carbohydrates and fats: potato chips, corn snacks, pretzels, crackers, cookies, doughnuts, sweet rolls, cake, and candy, as well as frozen dairy desserts and fresh and processed meat. Many of the latter are loaded with sodium, which encourages fluid retention.

Excellent natural sources for tryptophan are chicken, cheddar cheese, milk, tuna, turkey, soybeans, and products derived from soybean (such as tofu).

CARNITINE

This substance is also known as vitamin BT. It speeds up the burning of fat. Our body synthesizes carnitine, but must obtain the raw materials for its production from certain food sources. The best sources for this substance are yeast, milk, wheat germ and the muscle meats of lamb, beef, chicken and sheep. Vegetarian diets are usually deficient in this nutrient, as only negligible amounts of carnitine are contained in fruits and vegetables.

CHOLESTEROL

Cholesterol is a wax-like substance that is needed for the body's normal metabolism. It travels through the blood system in little protein "packages" called lipoproteins. Your body naturally produces all the cholesterol it needs. This is why you don't need any dietary cholesterol and should avoid foods that raise the cholesterol levels in your blood. If your cholesterol is too high, you are at greater risk of developing heart disease.

One type of cholesterol is low-density lipoprotein, or LDL. It is commonly referred to as "bad" cholesterol because it damages the arterial walls. High-density lipoprotein, or HDL, is called "good" cholesterol because it appears to protect the arteries from damage.

We should derive no more than ten percent of our daily calories from saturated fat, according to the American Heart Association. A reduction in saturated fat in our diet can easily be accomplished by substituting fish, poultry, lean meats, whole grain brands and cereals, fruits and vegetables, and dried peas and beans for foods high in fat.

Foods High in Saturated Fat

Beef
> Round steak
> Roast
> Porterhouse steak
> Ground beef, lean

Whole milk
Moist Cheese
Hot dogs
Lunchmeats
Doughnuts
Cake
Pork
> Chops

Ham
Sausage
Bacon
Butter
Ice Cream
Fried potatoes
2% milk
Potato chips
Nondairy coffee
    Creamer (coconut oil)

Low Saturated Fat Choices

Fruit
Vegetables
Turkey breast, roasted,
    baked, broiled, without skin
Chicken breast
roasted, baked, broiled, without skin
Fish, broiled, baked, poached
Skim milk
Low fat yogurt
1% cottage cheese
Safflower oil
Corn oil
Olive oil
Margarines made with polyunsaturated oils
Dried peas and beans
Pasta, without cheese or meat
Rice
Popcorn, air popped without butter
Whole grain breads

Oat bran actually lowers cholesterol slightly. Your physician can do a simple blood test to determine your cholesterol count. The lower the LDL and HDL ratio, the lower your risk to heart disease. Exercise has been shown to boost HLD.

- Total cholesterol level divided by HDL for men should equal 4.5 or less.
- Total cholesterol level divided by HDL for women should equal 3.6 or less.

Your total cholesterol count should be less than 180 mg/dl if you are under 20 and below 200 mg/dl over the age of 20. A borderline high risk level is from 200-239 mg/dl. Total cholesterol counts over 240 mg/dl is considered high risk for a heart attack.

Here are some very important facts about cholesterol:

- Men's Average HDL = 45 mg/dl.
- Women's Average HDL = 55 mg/dl.
- The higher the HDL, the lower the risk of heart disease.
- A HDL level lower than 35 mg/dl is a major risk factor for heart disease.

CATABOLIC FOODS

Catabolic foods are quite simply foods that break down fat and contain what are referred to as reversed calories. By reduced calories these foods burn fat rather than add fat. Anabolic foods function in quite the opposite manner.

A certain amount of body heat and energy in the form of calories is utilized in the process of digestion of any type of food. Let me illustrate this process with the digestion of a six-ounce piece of roast beef. Assuming it contains about 250 calories and burns up 80 calories during digestion, we are left with a net 170 calories which will be stored as fat, unless burned up through exercise or other physical activities.

A medium-sized orange may contain 70 calories, but requires

100 calories of energy to be digested. The result is a negative 30 calories, which will now activate a process of removing 30 calories of stored fat. In these two examples the roast beef represents an anabolic food, while the orange a catabolic food.

You will find that the majority of catabolic foods are rich in vitamins and minerals and have a very high water content. Many of them balance the acidity resulting from the removal of stored fat by providing an alkaline component to the body. Another advantage of catabolic foods is that some of them (lean meats, for example) stimulate the pancreas to produce a fat-dissolving hormone known as *glucagon.*

Since catabolic foods function to counter the effects of fattening anabolic foods, we can eat large amounts of the low calorie catabolic foods to reverse the effect of a high caloric meal

Here are examples of catabolic foods from the various food groups:

Fruits
apples
grapefruit
grapes
lemons
mangoes
cantaloupe
oranges
peaches
watermelon
blueberries
papaya
pineapple
strawberries
cherries
raspberries

Vegetables

broccoli
corn
onions
peas
cucumbers
lettuce
radishes
pumpkin
turnips
okra
peppers
rhubarb
spinach
asparagus
cabbage
tomato
beets
cauliflower
garlic
sauerkraut
carrots
celery
kale

Fish
crab
oyster
sea bass
flounder
shrimp
cod steaks
mussel
lobster

Most people assume it is best to fast or to eat just a few calories to lose weight. It is far superior to eat fat-burning catabolic foods to achieve this goal.

It is best not to drink water during meals but drink either thirty minutes before or following a meal. To permanently lose weight and maintain your ideal weight I recommend 2/3 catabolic to 1/3 anabolic foods in your diet. Drinking water alone several times a day facilitates fat elimination.

INSULIN—THE MAIN OBSTACLE TO WEIGHT LOSS

Insulin is produced by the pancreas and it literally tells your body when to eat, transports food energy to needy cells and is responsible for the storage of unused energy as fat.

When insulin levels are high the body cannot efficiently burn stored fat. The key is to keep this insulin level in a zone so its levels don't shoot up. High-density carbohydrates found in bread, rice, potatoes, grains, cereal and pasta result in a quick boost to insulin levels. We can prevent this from occurring by eating low-density carbohydrates found in fruits and vegetables, which are also catabolic.

Another way to slow down the rate in which carbohydrates enter the bloodstream is to eat monosaturated fats, such as avocados, cashews, pistachio nuts, almonds, cashews, macadamia nuts, fish oil and olive oil. It is best to include some form of monosaturated fats in every meal and snack. As I previously stated, our diet should contain 30 percent fat—monosaturated fat.

Insulin levels are stimulated by eating carbohydrates alone, so always include other food groups when eating carbohydrates. Protein lowers insulin levels, whereas caffeine stimulates insulin production. Aerobic exercise, such as biking, swimming, walking and working out on a treadmill reduce the levels of insulin.

CHAPTER 5

EXERCISE—A LITTLE GOES A LONG WAY

Our ancestors had no need for formal exercise. Mild to moderate physical activity was required for survival. In order to obtain food they had to gather fruits and berries or run down prey. Farming was later developed, but this also required much physical exertion.

Today we have supermarkets, cars and a sedentary lifestyle. Exercise doesn't have to be tedious or strenuous. Both our mind and body benefit from regular, moderate exercise that can be quite enjoyable.

Although physically active people outlive inactive people at any age, twenty-five percent of adult Americans are completely sedentary. At least fifty percent of the U.S. population would benefit from being more active.

It is next to impossible to attain the goal of becoming healthy, lean and strong if you do not incorporate *regular* exercise into your daily activities. In addition to the health benefits, exercise improves the quantity as well as the quality of your life.

Inactive people have twice the risk of coronary heart disease and cancer as those who are physically active. Regular physical activity directly reduces rates of heart disease, high blood pressure, noninsulin-dependent diabetes, osteoporosis, breast and colon cancer, and depression and other forms of mental illness.

Exercise can help osteoarthritis sufferers delay or avoid knee surgery. For example, aerobic exercise (i.e., brisk walking) or strengthening exercises (i.e., weight lifting) in 30- to 45-minute sessions, three times a week, has reduced pain and increased ease performing everyday tasks such as climbing stairs for patients with osteoarthritis. It is believed that exercise helps relieve arthritis pain by strengthening the muscles around the knee that help it stay in the correct position and by increasing brain chemicals that block pain.

Exercise during the day can help you sleep better at night. To help sleep, exercise should be done earlier in the day, well before supper time. Bike riding, brisk walking or moderate aerobic exercise has proven to be the best for solving sleep difficulties.

Other advantages of regular exercise include:

- Relief of tension.
- Increased longevity.
- Increases and maintains muscle tissue.
- Lowers blood pressure.
- Increased vitality.
- Decreases excess body fat.
- Curbed appetite.
- Increased mental alertness and productivity.
- Lowers your cholesterol.
- Lowers our bodies set point (the pre set level of fat the body attempts to maintain regardless of the number of calories consumed) and aid in losing weight permanently.
- Makes you look thinner even if there is no change in your body weight. Since a pound of lean muscle takes up less space than a pound of fat, you will lose inches around your stomach region.
- It is the best protection against regaining weight lost before.
- Decreases your vulnerability to binge eating.
- Reduces depression and stress.

To be effective we need to exercise at least three times a week for thirty minutes at each day that we participate in some physical activity.

There are two main types of exercise, aerobic and isotonic (nonaerobic). To engage in aerobic exercise, your body must consume oxygen. Swimming, walking, biking and jogging are common examples. Your body is forced to breathe steadily in and out and steadily with aerobic regimens.

Isotonic exercises focus on strength building and require contraction of a set of muscles, usually while you are moving a joint. Examples of this category include weight lifting, stretching, archery, horseshoes, shuffleboard and other mild recreational sports. Here are some warming up and cooling down exercises that should precede a regular workout:

- *Sit on the floor with one leg bent towards the thigh of the other leg. This other leg is stretched straight out with your toes pointing up. Lean forward while keeping your back straight and slowly grasp your toes.*
- *While in this sitting position extend your left leg out and cross your right leg over it. Draw your right knee back with your left arm.*
- *Lie on the floor on your back with both knees bent. Close your eyes, take a deep breath and slowly exhale. Slide one knee forward till your leg is flat. Breathe deeply. Then bend it again. Repeat movement with other leg. Tighten both fists, then let go. Next, take a deep breath. Exhale slowly. Then shrug as you inhale and relax your shoulders as you exhale. Roll your head slowly from side to side.*
- *Still lying down with knees flexed, slowly bring your right knee as close to your chest as you can. Put your foot on the floor and slide your leg flat. Return to flexed position. Now repeat with the other leg.*
- *Lying on your back with your arms outstretched twist your hips to the left and tuck your right calf under your left knee.*
- *Now straighten your left leg and extend the right leg. Try to bring your toes to your left hand.*
- *Kneel on your left leg with your right foot flat on the ground, pointing out in the same direction as your right shoulder. Lean forward towards your right leg with your left hand by your side. Now switch legs and repeat this stretch.*

- *To warm up for aerobic dancing, extend your arms. Make big circles, keeping your head centered between them. Reach towards the floor and to the ceiling. Keep your lower body still. Breathe deeply.*
- *Another movement consists of quickly shifting your weight from one leg to the other. The movement is light and bouncy. Arms swing in the same direction as weight change.*
- *Jog forward 3 steps, then, with hands on hips, bring one knee up. Jog back 3 steps, then bring the other knee up. Alternate the starting leg and repeat this procedure.*

CALISTHENICS

Although not aerobic exercises, calisthenics strengthen your muscles, give you staying power and help you to become flexible. Avoid holding your breath while you are doing calisthenics. Do each of these exercises four times daily.

ARM EXTENSIONS
- *Stand with your legs shoulder-width apart and bend over at the waist. Keep your elbows close to your side and as high as possible. Extend your arms towards your back, as if you were trying to touch the ceiling.*

SIDE BENDS
- *Stand with your feet shoulder-width apart and your right hand behind your head. Your left hand is hanging down your left side.*
- *Bend to the left and then to the right.*
- *Alternate hands and repeat this exercise.*

HALF SQUATS
- *Stand with your feet shoulder-width apart. Bend your knees and lean back slightly in an attempt to keep your shoulders behind your heels.*
- *Bend and straighten 5 times.*

TOE RAISES
- *Stand with your feet in a comfortable position. Raise yourself up on your toes for a count of 3, then lower yourself. Repeat this 15 times.*

RAG DOLL STRETCH
- *Stand with your feet shoulder-width apart and bend at the waist so that your hands hang loosely towards the floor.*
- *Try to keep your back flat and just hang.*

NECK ROTATOR
- *Stand with your feet in a wide stance. Bend forward at the waist and with your hands on your knees.*
- *Turn your head slowly from side to side as you attempt to look up at the ceiling.*

ARCH UPS
- *Place your arms by your sides for support as you lie flat on your back.*
- *Bend your knees with your feet flat on the floor and raise your hip up as high as you can.*

FOR THE STOMACH
(Lie on your back with knees bent and your feet securely tucked under a chair. Extend your arms over your head.)
1. *Swing your arms up and towards your knees while raising your head and shoulders off the floor.*
2. *Touch your hands to your knees (right-right, left-left).*
3. *Lower your head and shoulders to the floor as you return your arms to the starting position.*
4. *Repeat Steps 1-3 and twist to the left.*
5. *Repeat Steps 1-3 and twist to the right.*
6. *Repeat Steps 1-5 from 2-10 times.*

FOR THE STOMACH AND BUTTOCKS
(Still on all fours)
1. *Raise your right knee to your chest.*
2. *Swing your right leg back and lift.*
3. *Repeat 4-20 times.*
4. *Repeat Steps 1-3 with the left leg.*

STOMACH AND HIP FLEXERS
(Lie down, resting on elbows)
1. *Bring both feet toward hips.*
2. *Raise your knees toward your chest while bringing your feet off the floor.*
3. *Return your feet to the floor and straighten your legs.*
4. *Repeat 4-20 times.*
As the exercise becomes easier, try to keep your feet off the floor for the entire set.

FOR THE HIPS
(Get down on all fours.)
1. *Raise your right knee to the side (hip height) 4-20 times.*
2. *Lower your knee to the floor.*
3. *Raise your left knee to the side (hip height) 4-20 times.*
4. *Lower it to the floor.*
As the exercise becomes easier, extend your leg out and then return before lowering it.

You are working at moderate to high intensity if you find yourself breathing hard, working up a visible sweat and feeling your muscles pushing and pulling during your workout.

Getting your body up and moving as often and as energetically as possible is the key to becoming physically fit. The safest and most reliable way to raise your intensity of exercise is to increase frequency and duration.

Exercise will not work against your weight goal. You may eat a little more than those with a sedentary lifestyle, but you will lose a lot more calories in the end. In addition, exercise speeds up our metabolism. Always select a form of exercise that you enjoy, and you will work at a moderate rate that is comfortable at your fitness level.

EXAMPLES OF OTHER DAILY EXERCISES

*   Gardening—Digging, hoeing, spading and weeding uses 350 calories for the average woman and 390 calories an hour for the average man.

- Mowing the Lawn—You burn up 145 calories an hour steering a ride-on mower and 250 calories per hour using a self-drive mower.
- Preparing Dinner—A woman burns up about 105 calories and a man 135 per hour.
- Painting a Wall—You can burn up between 165 to 210 calories per hour.
- Washing Windows—House work such as this burns up between 195 to 250 calories per hour
- Hand Carpentry—Hand sawing burns up 305 to 390 calories per hour.
- Doing the Laundry—In addition to clean clothes, you will burn 190 to 245 calories an hour.

To get the most out of exercising and protect your body, I suggest:
- Never drink alcohol before exercising.
- Drink more fluids if you notice your urine is dark. This is an indication of dehydration.
- Have a light meal that is high in carbohydrates before exercising.
- Breathe out as you tense your muscles, while inhaling as these muscles relax. Establish a regular rhythm for your breathing and use that rhythm to pace yourself.
- Always keep your body in alignment to protect your back. Refrain from slumping, slouching and arching your back.
- Weigh yourself before exercising and drink enough water to return your weight to its previous level following exercising.
- Keep your knees and elbows slightly flexed and do not lock your joints.
- Exercises at least every other day, preferably daily, for at least 10 minutes, working up to a regular workout of half an hour or more several times a week.
- Establish a sensible goal based on your current fitness level, and only gradually increase intensity and duration over a period of weeks.

- Always warm up prior to exercising and cool down following physical activity. This will prevent or lessen soreness and stiffness the following day. Warm-ups and cool-downs and stretches are vital. A 10-minute walk or slow bike ride to wherever you're exercising, or a few minutes of light jogging in place will serve for a warm-up, if you don't enjoy the previous exercises I presented. This will gradually increase your blood flow and heart rate and condition you for your workout.

- Always aim for steady resistance rather than jerking, flailing, or pounding movements, which can injure muscles.

- Design your regimen to work on as many muscle groups as possible. The more large muscles you use, the more calories you burn now and the more new muscle you build.

- Decrease your intake of coffee and other caffeinated beverages.

- Follow manufacturer's recommendations on any equipment you use and dress appropriately. Your clothes should fit loosely and allow for a free range of motion.

- Get approval from your physician before initiating any form of exercise regimen.

- Never stand still immediately after high-intensity exercise. always stretch and cool down before stopping.

- If pain or other discomfort is experienced, you probably didn't spend enough time warming up or cooling down. You may have worked yourself too long or too hard. Stop immediately if you feel labored breathing, dizziness, loss of coordination, tightness or pain in your chest, nausea or vomiting, heart rate irregularity, or a stabbing, tearing, or wrenching pain. Consult a physician as soon as possible, and get a medical okay before resuming exercise.

- To make exercise fun workout to music and engage in regular physical activity with friends.

- Internal training often results in a shorter period of time to get into shape. This consists of alternating three to five minutes of high-intensity movement with up to three minutes of moderate movement.
- To maintain your interest in exercising, vary your regimen. For example, consider alternating between swimming one day and walking or other aerobic activities the following day.
- For cold weather workouts wear a hat or hood to keep heat within your body. Heat actually rises and leaves your body through your head. Also, warm up and cool down indoors.

YOGA AND WEIGHT LOSS

Yogic asanas have been utilized for both relaxation and weight loss for thousands of years. Proper, purposeful relaxation offers the greatest amount of renewed strength in the shortest length of time. Try these asanas, or poses, to relax.

CORPSE POSE

Lie face up with your feet extended. Remain motionless with a sense of feeling of sinking down like a corpse. Gradually relax every muscle of the body by concentrating on each individually, from the tip of the toe to the end of the skull. Exercise absolute resignation of will by trying to forget the existence of your body and detaching yourself from it. Hold this posture until you feel restored.

SNAKE POSE

Lie on your stomach, with your legs stretched and toes pointed outward. Keep your arms at your sides, with palms down, and your forehead on the floor. Then, slowly raise your head and neck upward and backward.

When your head and neck are slightly raised, plant your hands on both sides of the abdomen. Inhale, and gradually raise your thorax and the upper part of your abdomen by increasing the angle between your hands and rising shoulders. From the navel downward, your body should remain fixed to the ground. Only the upper portion of your body should be raised. Work towards this pose gradually, avoiding muscular strain or "jerkiness" in your efforts to raise the upper part of your body. As you practice this pose, you will feel the pressure on your spinal column gradually working down the vertebrae until you feel a deep pressure at the coccyx.

At first, concentrate on the posture. Having achieved the correct pose, exhale and return to the starting position. Lower yourself slowly. In contrast to the pressure which you felt as you entered this posture, you will experience a feeling of relief along your spine as you lower yourself.

After the pose has been mastered, follow this procedure: (1) Raise thorax and inhale for three seconds; (2) maintain pose, retaining your breath for six seconds; (3) return to starting position, while exhaling for three seconds; (4) repeat five times in a minute.

MOUNTAIN POSE

This asana has been specially designed to maintain your ideal weight.

First assume a Semi-Lotus pose by sitting on the floor with your legs stretched out. Bend the right leg slowly and fold it upon itself. Using your hands, place the right heel at the root of the thigh so that its sole is turned upwards and your foot is stretched over the left groin. Now bend the left leg and fold it upon itself with your hands placing the left heel over the root of the right thigh. Your ankles should cross each other, while your heel-ends touch closely.

Now, slowly raise your hands upward and above the head. Keep your palms pressed together. If it is easier, interlace your fingers. Finally, stretch upward as if to touch some object directly above your head. Keep your arms close to your ears, your head erect, your back straight, and pull your abdomen in. While inhaling, raise the upper part of your body to its maximum height. Make sure your elbows and wrists are in a straight line.

Maintain this slightly stretched, upright position between breaths. During this exercise, keep your eyes fixed on some object before you and keep your mind at ease.

For maximum benefits, the movements and breathing should be in harmony with actions as shown in the following instructions: (1) In a sitting pose, raise arms and inhale for three seconds; (2) maintain pose and *try to retain breath for six seconds; (3) return to starting position, exhale for three seconds. Repeat this pose five times to a minute without pausing.*

This posture tenses and pulls all the abdominal and pelvic muscles, strengthens and straightens the muscles of the back and also stretches and exercises the usually inactive waist zone. One of its most evident benefits will be the reduction of fat and flabby abdominal tissue. However, it must be followed consistently for one minute, both in the morning and evening.

There are four dynamic variations of this pose. They are: (1) Swaying forward; (2) leaning backward; (3) bending to the right; (4) bending to the left. These variations should be utilized during a six-second breathing pause. Instead of maintaining the perpendicular position while stretching, vary it by making the movements on the four sides and alternately. Gradually increase the retention of your breath to nine seconds, which will permit four movements to a minute.

WEIGHT LIFTING

Weight lifting does tone and shape muscles and build strength. This is not an aerobic exercise. To obtain the greatest benefit from weight lifting, sports experts suggest the following:

- Focus on building your muscle bulk for the first two months. Have as your goal the ability to do 12-20 repetitions of a lift without undue strain.
- Work on endurance for the next two months. You should be able to do 40-50 repetitions without stopping.
- Lastly, build your strength. Move on to heavier weights that challenge you to do 2-6 repetitions. Increase the amount of the weights as your strength increases.

Exercise can be accomplished in one of two ways. You can either schedule specific blocks of time for working out, or you can incorporate physical activity while performing daily tasks. Here are some examples of the latter category:

- Practice short neck and shoulder exercises periodically if you sit all day.
- Instead of calling neighbors or colleagues, walk to their home or office.
- Refrain from moving walkways or trams at theme parks and airports. Walk and keep a brisk pace.
- Instead of taking a coffee break, go out for a brisk walk.
- When reading memos or reports in your office, pace up and down.
- Whenever possible avoid labor saving devices and engage in physical activity instead.
- Use stairs instead of elevators and escalators. Go out of your way to obtain additional exercise. For example, use a rest room or copy machine two or three floors up or down from your office.
- Take a bicycle to work or to run errands.
- Walk in to establishments that have drive-through windows.
- Change your nightly routine to incorporate exercise in place of watching television or reading for some of your entertainment. For example, go for a walk, play tennis, swim or go cycling. Consider playing catch with your child or dog.
- Exercise while watching television, doing the dishes, ironing and housecleaning.
- When going shopping park at the far end of the parking lot or mall and walk the extra distance.
- Instead of using shopping carts at a supermarket, carry your own bags. This burns extra calories and builds up muscle tissue.

Let us consider some of the more common and easily available forms of exercise.

WALKING

This is an activity that is low on stress to our joints that tones the lower body muscles and is an excellent cardiovascular activity.

TIPS FOR WALKING

- Use the best running shoes you can afford. Buy these in a store that specializes in running equipment. Select shoes that are about 1/4 inch longer than your longest toe. The sole must be flexible and the heel counter (the part that wraps around the back of your heel) should be firm.
- Let your arms swing freely.
- Walk on your whole foot.
- Avoid walking when it is very hot or cold.
- Begin with a 15 to 20 minute walk and walk at a slower pace for the first several minutes as a warm up.
- Walk with your head erect and your stomach in.

SWIMMING

Swimming results in about the same fat loss as cycling but less than walking or jogging. We increase our cardiovascular endurance, build muscle strength and use more muscles than any other form of exercise when we engage in swimming.

Try these exercises while in your pool.

PENDULUM SWITCH
- *Float on your back with your arms at your sides. Bend your hips and reach forward with your arms.*
- *Keep your knees straight and extend your legs back. Now move in a prone position like a jack knife and slowly return to a float position on your stomach with hands straight out.*

PUSH-UPS

- *With your hands on the edge of the pool, shoulder width apart, stand with your body facing the wall of the pool. Straighten your elbows and lift your body out of the water.*
- *Hold this position for at least three seconds.*

REAR PUSH-UPS

- *Stand in waist-deep water with your back against the wall of the pool. With your fingers pointing towards the water, place your hands on the edge of the pool close to your sides.*
- *Now straighten your elbows and lift our body out of the water. Maintain this position for three seconds. Bring your legs into an "L" position after a few repetitions.*

SIT-UPS

- *Float on your back with your hands holding onto the edge of the pool. Bend your knees and move them in the direction of your chest. Extend your legs again.*
- *For a more vigorous exercise, place your bent knees and calves on the pool deck. Float on your back while supporting your head with your hands.*
- *Tuck your chin up to your chest and lie back.*

CRAB STRETCH

- *Place your back against the pool wall and the soles of your feet flat against the same wall.*
- *Arch your back while holding onto the pool's edge with your hands and straighten your legs as much as possible. Keep your head looking straight ahead and slowly return to the original position.*

LEG SWING

- *Place both arms on the edge of the pool with your back to the wall. Lift your legs to an "L" position and keep this position as you twist your body and swing your legs from right to left.*

AEROBICS

Any form of aerobic activity burns calories at a high rate and is an excellent type of cardiovascular regimen. To be classified as aerobic, the activity must be vigorous and sustained for 15 to 30 minutes. The machines on the market and in gyms tone primarily lower body muscles. Such devices as Stairmaster, skiing machines, rowing machines, climbers and Stepmaster are examples. Non machine examples of aerobic exercises are bicycling, swimming, jogging, some calisthenics, dancing and brisk walking. Unless there is continuous movement, golf, tennis and bowling do not qualify as aerobic activity.

JOGGING

Jogging requires the least amount of time for the greatest caloric expenditure. It tones lower body muscles and is a high quality cardiovascular activity. You need to be careful not to aggravate arthritis symptoms. In addition, jogging places high stress on the spine, hips, knees and ankles, which may lead to injury.

TENNIS/HANDBALL/RACQUETBALL

These are excellent cardiovascular (aerobic) exercises and calorie burners only if you are constantly moving. The muscles of the upper and lower body are toned as a result of these activities.

SKIING

The highest rate of fat and caloric burning of any popular exercise is from cross-country uphill skiing. Muscles throughout the entire body are worked when we engage in skiing.

CYCLING

This activity tones the lower body muscles, is an excellent cardiovascular workout and moderately burns calories.

GOLF

Golfing only slightly tones the back and upper arm muscles. Most of the fat loss and cardiovascular benefits are primarily due to walking the course. Even this is compromised by the use of golf carts.

A proper exercise program begins with relaxation techniques such as meditation, breathing approaches or self-hypnosis. We will discuss these methods in greater detail in the next two chapters.

Following relaxation, warming up and stretching exercises are recommended. Next conduct your workout and end with a cooldown period. This process assists in releasing tension and stress, in addition to help to strengthen and build muscles and burn fat.

Aerobic activity triggers the release of serotonic and endorphins. Both of these naturally produced substances bring on a feel-good effect, or natural high. They assist in eliminating depression and pain.

To further enhance your de-stressing goal, schedule exercise five or six hours before retiring. Exercising too close to going to bed may cause insomnia. Other tips to prevent insomnia is to refrain from drinking alcohol within a few hours of bedtime. Initially you may feel sleepy, but most commonly you will awaken about two hours later. A better solution is to have a warm glass of milk and/or a piece of whole-grain toast with honey. The milk contains tryptophan, and coupled with retiring and arising at the same time every day (including weekends), your insomnia will quickly disappear.

Cramps following or during exercising can be eliminated by raising your arms over your head and breathing deeply. This expands your diaphragm and allows you to take in more oxygen at a faster rate. Cramping is due to a lack of oxygen.

There are many inexpensive ways of beginning an exercise program. For example, you can rent or purchase workout videotapes from your local video store. Many high schools have evening exercise classes for adults. Lastly, you can buy a single well-made exercise machine. The cost of this is a one-time expense, and is far more economical than health club dues.

CHAPTER 6

USING MIND-BODY TECHNIQUES TO LOSE

WEIGHT

It has been well established throughout this century that our thoughts, feelings, actions and moods significantly affect our health. This mind-body interaction shapes our sense of well-being and overall happiness. One result of this connection may be weight problems.

The purpose of this chapter is to introduce you to the concept of using mind-body techniques to establish a positive self-image and permanently eliminate the tendency to overeat.

We can use mind-body methods to:

- Eliminate anxiety and depression
- Ease insomnia
- Improve our immune system
- Block pain
- Lower blood pressure and cholesterol levels
- Relieve stress
- Extend our lives
- Lose weight permanently and naturally

Let me be perfectly clear about these advantages. Mind-body techniques have been shown to alter our body chemistry and treat or prevent a host of diseases. For example, consider these findings:

- Optimistic men have less chronic illness in later life.
- Heart disease may be prevented by reducing anger and hostility feelings.
- Headaches, arthritis, hay fever, colds, warts, constipation, angina, insomnia, and pain after surgery, have been helped by positive beliefs and expectations.
- Imagery techniques have been shown to boost our immune system and fight many diseases from the common cold to cancer and AIDS.
- The production of stress hormones can be reduced following a massage.
- Cholesterol levels, stomach acid, endorphin levels and immune system functions may be changed to our benefit through positive expectations about treatment regimens.
- Hypnosis has helped diabetics stabilize blood sugar levels and hemophiliacs to control their bleeding.

These alternative medicine approaches include meditation, hypnosis, yoga, visual imagery, affirmations, breathing exercises and mindfulness, to name a few. They are most effective when practiced on a regular basis.

You take a more active role in maintaining both your physical and psychological health with these approaches. That is why I refer to them as a form of psychic empowerment. The only real side effects are positive feelings of well-being, better moods and improved self-image. These methods are extremely effective in prevention of mental/physical disease.

OPTIMISM

One of the easiest ways to practice mind-body technique is to simply become more optimistic about life. Throughout our daily activities we use a form of self-talk that is responsible for most of our moods and feelings. We may not be consciously aware of these negative thoughts, but they most certainly exert a significant influence on our moods.

Do we not feel frustrated or angry when a spouse forgets a birthday or anniversary, or someone is late for an appointment with us? Feelings of depression can accompany the loss of money, a death in the family or a divorce. Many people respond to a traffic ticket or a letter from the IRS with intense feelings of anxiety.

If you constantly say to yourself, "I'm not very bright," or "I'm too fat," you are practicing a negative form of self-talk. Positive attitudes are not that difficult to adopt. Try on a new pair of rose-colored glasses, even if it requires a distortion of the world in which you live.

Since none of us perceive the outside world with complete accuracy, all self-talk is based on distortions and illusions. Our brain interprets the data it receives from our five senses. Just as a newspaper editorial reflects the position of the paper, our mind sees what it wants to see. We may as well slant this distortion to the positive side. You will find the effects far healthier.

Optimistic thinking is characterized by the following paradigms:

- Focus on the present.
- Always look on the bright side.
- Expect good thing to happen—always expect the best.
- Be positive about the future. See it in terms of what can be done rather than what cannot.
- Perceive all setbacks as challenges to be overcome and learning opportunities.
- Recall only positive past events.
- View all obstacles as temporary and good events as permanent.
- Attribute good events to your own efforts.
- Generalize positive outcomes to your entire life. Statements such as, "my whole life is working great just as I planned it" can be made following a success.

Optimists eliminate the words "should," "ought to," and "must" from their vocabulary. They never say, "I should be thin." Words such as "want" or "could" are used instead. This removes the burden of guilt and represents an intention upon which you choose to act.

AFFIRMATIONS

Repeating positive statements known as affirmations represent another method of reprogramming our subconscious (more on this in chapter 6). These statements become just as powerful as their negative predecessors over time.

The best way to practice affirmations is to create positive statements about yourself and place them in the present tense. Next, set aside a few minutes each day to repeat these statements out loud or to yourself. These statements should be written down. They can be used during visual imagery exercises, meditation or self-hypnosis.

- I am in control of my eating habit.
- I am confident and motivated to lose weight.
- I create my own reality.
- I can relax at any time I choose.
- I deserve success in all my endeavors.
- I am losing weight steadily every day.
- I unconditionally love and accept myself.
- I have a calm mind and body.

MUSIC

Music exerts quite an effect upon our behavior. Fast beats make us aroused and alert, slow, quiet music calms and relaxes us, high-pitched music comes across as playful and happy and low-pitched music is associated with serious or sad moods.

Nature sounds can be very soothing, renewing and relaxing. Sounds emanating from the ocean, the chirping of birds, rain, the wind rustling through trees, the chatter of squirrels and so on have a definite effect upon us.

Aerobics classes always use music to dance by. Music may facilitate your motivation to exercise, increase endurance, regulates breathing and gets you in tune with your body. Some upbeat and fast tempo music makes you feel less tired. I always incorporate New Age music on my hypnosis sessions and the self-hypnosis and meditation tapes I give my patients.

One way to select music that is best suited to you is to listen to a variety of music styles. At this time, record which types make you feel happy, sad, energized or relaxed. Now begin listening to these pieces when you feel moody and note your responses.

Healing with sound and chanting has been practiced since ancient times. All forms of religion use music in their services. Lullabies have assisted children in falling asleep for thousands of years.

Music that is used in combination with guided imagery facilitates psychological and spiritual growth. Psychosomatic disorders of all types, including headaches, digestive problems, pain, anxiety and depression have been successfully treated with music.

RELAXATION RESPONSES

Through the use of self-hypnosis (see chapter 6) meditation, breathing exercises, deep muscle relaxation, yoga and visual imagery, you can learn to relax your body and refocus your mind.

Some of the immediate advantages of relaxation techniques are:

- Lowered breathing rates
- Slower heartbeat
- Lowered blood pressure
- Slowed basic metabolic rate
- Muscle relaxation
- Focused concentration
- A calm mind and body

A simple way to begin this relaxation approach is to focus all of your attention on the outside world. Select one sound or smell with your eyes closed and say to yourself, "I am aware of _____." Next shift your attention to your internal world of physical sensations and feelings. Say to yourself, "I am now aware of _____." You will most commonly observe that the previous external awareness is now replaced by your inner focus.

As another exercise, sit or lie down and let your mind scan your body with your eyes closed. Observe any sensations from your breathing to your stomach gurgling without judging them. During this body scan pause for a moment at each body part or organ.

Note any tenseness and begin to use affirmations to suggest relaxation in these tense muscles. Allow at least 15 minutes for this exercise and repeat it several times during the next week.

There are many activities that we enjoy that can facilitate a state of relaxation. Some examples are:

- Observe the clouds.
- View a funny movie or television show.
- Play with your pet.
- Get a massage.
- Take a relaxing walk.
- Do some arts and crafts.
- Go to the ocean or a park.
- Mentally recall a favorite vacation.

BREATHING EXERCISES

Relaxing our body is a natural consequence of proper breathing. Breathing mirrors our emotions. We gasp at amazement, sigh with relief and choke with sadness, do we not? Anger results in irregular breathing and fear brings this process to a quick halt.

We cannot be both tense and relaxed at the same time. Proper use of our breathing can be a powerful way to gain control over stress and our emotions. Feelings of dizziness, light-headedness or faint, while practicing these exercises indicate you are breathing too quickly or deeply. If this occurs, simply breathe normally for a few moments and those effects will pass.

As children we exhibit stomach or diaphragmatic breathing, during which our stomach rises with in-breaths and falls with out-breaths. Chest breathing replaces this pattern as adults. This un-healthy "stomach in", "chest out" shallow and rapid breathing pat-tern is more characteristic of anxiety and tension.

To relearn this natural stomach breathing style try this simple exercise:

1. *Lie down on your back, close your eyes and place your hands just below your navel.*
2. *Visualize a balloon inside your stomach that fills with air during each inhalation and shrinks as air escapes from it during exhalation.*
3. *Feel your hands gently rise with each in-breath and descend during your out-breath.*

Focus on the sensations and sounds associated with this form of breathing.

Frequent sighing or yawning suggest your lungs may not be receiving enough oxygen. The ancient yogins of India knew all about the value of proper breathing techniques. Their holy scrip-tures contain specific exercises of breathing and meditation. Here is an example of a yoga breathing method:

1. *Stand erect, raise your arms simultaneously up from your sides until they are outstretched and parallel to the ground. As you do this take a deep breath and hold it.*
2. *While holding the breath bring your arms down in front of you so that they form an X with your hands pointing at the ground. As you do this imagine that you are pulling down great weights. This will give a firm tone to the muscles of your arms, shoulders and back.*

3. *Hold the arms in the crossed downward position for the count of eight and continue to hold your breath as well. As you do this imagine your breath going to the base of the spine in the form of energy.*
4. *After the count of eight, exhale, relax your arms, letting them drop to your sides as you resume your original erect posture.*

Perform this exercise three times at first, but after three weeks increase it to seven times each exercise period.

This is a more advanced breathing technique:

1. *Sit in a straight back chair with both feet flat on the floor and your spine held in an erect position.*
2. *Breathe in slowly through the left nostril. If necessary, hold the right nostril closed by pressing it with your finger. After a little practice you will find that you will be able to direct the flow of your breath into the proper nostril without blocking off the other.*
3. *Now hold your breath to the count of ten and as you do feel it energizing the center at the base of your spine.*
4. *Now cover your left nostril and allow your breath to escape slowly through the right nostril to the count of eight. As you do this visualize the breath leaving the base of the spine, traveling up its right side and out the right nostril.*
5. *Now repeat the process but start this time by covering the left nostril and inhaling for the count of four through the right nostril. As you do this feel the breath going from the throat down the right side of your spine to its base.*
6. *Hold your breath at the base of the spine for the count of ten and then permit it to escape up the left side of your spine and out the left nostril while you count to eight.*

Finally, try this breathing method that incorporates visual imagery:

1. *Lie down in a comfortable position. Establish a steady and rhythmic breathing pattern.*

2. *Imagine your breath rising up the body through the bones of the legs and finally forced out of them. Repeat this step but now focus on the bones of the arms, then the skull, the stomach and genitals.*
3. *Visualize your breath rising up the backbone as you inhale, and descending down it as you exhale. See your breath being inhaled and exhaled through every pore in your skin.*
4. *Now send your breath as in the previous step to your forehead, back of the head, base of the brain, heart, solar plexus, navel region and genitals.*
5. *Finally, exhale all of your breath from your lungs and relax.*

MUSCLE RELAXATION

The principle behind muscle relaxation in mind-body approaches is that whatever relaxes your muscles will also relax your mind. Tensing and relaxing each muscle group one at a time will result in a progressive relaxation of your entire body, while calming the mind at the same time.

For this exercise you are going to tense each muscle group for five seconds and focus on this sensation. This is followed by breathing deeply and immediately releasing this tension so the muscle goes completely limp. At this time you are to observe the difference between the tense sensation and the relaxed state for twenty seconds. Each muscle group is to be tensed and relaxed twice.

1. *Lie down on your back on a soft surface. Clench your left fist and keep it tense for five seconds. Notice the feeling in all of your muscles of your fingers, hand and forearm.*
2. *Breathe deeply and immediately relax your hand and arm, noticing the looseness in your right hand and compare this sensation to the previous tensed one for twenty seconds.*
3. *Repeat these steps once again and do this same exercise with your right hand.*
4. *Now repeat steps 1 through 3 with your arms and upper arms.*

5. *Now straighten your thigh muscles and press your heels against the surface beneath you. Repeat steps 1 to 3.*

6. *Tense your calf muscles by pointing your toes down and curling them. Repeat steps 1 to 3.*

7. *Bend your toes up towards your head and produce tension in your shin region. Repeat steps 1 to 3.*

8. *Pull your stomach in and hold it for five seconds. Repeat steps 1 to 3.*

9. *Squeeze your buttocks together for five seconds. Repeat steps 1 to 3.*

10. *Repeat these procedures with your shoulders by shrugging them, pressing your shoulder blades together and arching your back.*

11. *For the neck press your head back as far as you comfortably can, hold, then relax.*

12. *Pull your chin down as if attempting to touch your chest, hold, then relax.*

13. *Use movements such as wrinkling your forehead, frowning, closing your eyes tightly, wrinkling your nose, clenching your jaws, pressing your tongue against the roof of your mouth and pursing your lips. For the rest of the body, always repeat steps 1 to 3.*

When you have completed this exercise with two repetitions, feel the complete sensation of relaxation permeating your entire body. Savor this feeling and take several long, deep breaths just before getting up. This procedure allows you to quickly scan the body, locate tense areas and relax them.

MINDFULNESS

Throughout the day most of us function robotically preoccupied with some thought, while we carry out routine functions. This may consist of making a sandwich, driving, doing the laundry and so on. Our mind is focused on the past or future while we seem to ignore the present moment.

Keeping your attention in the present moment is what we term mindfulness. This method is an attitude towards living, not just a relaxation technique. Mindfulness is a form of meditation that is at least 2500 years old, but is applicable today.

Practicing this exercise brings about an inner balance of mind and body that fosters clarity, compassion and allows you to globally assess the world around you. Since there is no judgment involved, negative emotions, such as anger or fear, are prevented from developing.

The goal of mindfulness is simply to observe and accept life as it is. This enables all of us to become calmer, more confident and far better able to deal with life.

Before beginning a meditative exercise, practice observing your next meal. Try this series of steps:

- Note how the food looks, its color, texture and even its smell.
- Focus on the feelings you have about eating this particular meal.
- Feel the food as it enters your mouth.
- While chewing slowly pay attention to its taste and texture.
- Keep centered on your intention to swallow this food. Notice all of the sensations accompanying the actual mechanism of swallowing.
- Observe how you feel following this meal.

You can apply this method to observing your associations of food with negative trigger zones, such as anxiety, anger, depression, watching television, frustration and so on.

Here is a simple mindfulness meditation.

1. *Sit comfortably with your eyes closed and back, neck and head straight. Focus on your breathing. Just observe it without attempting to alter it.*
2. *Your mind will most likely wander off and think of a memory or something else. Simply observe these thoughts and slowly refocus your attention to your breathing.*

3. *Each time another thought enters your mind, refrain from judging it; just observe it and return to your breathing.*
4. *Continue this for five minutes and then open up your eyes.*

You may lengthen this exercise to ten, fifteen or twenty minutes in the future.

CONCENTRATION MEDITATION

This form of meditation uses a mantra. Many types of mantras exist from religious prayers to a simple word. The word "OM" is the most well known mantra.

In concentration meditation we are focusing our mind by concentrating on a mantra or our breathing. All this time a nonjudgmental and detached observer's view of our mind's thoughts is taken. As you breathe in and with each exhalation repeat your mantra.

1. *Sit comfortably and breath deeply. Each time you breathe out say the word om. Om. Om. Om. Breathe softly and normally, but now do not concentrate on your breathing.*
2. *Now repeat your mantra (or om) in your mind. Just think of saying it. Do not actually move your lips. Just think of it. Do not concentrate on your breathing. Let the mantra repeat itself in your mind. Do not force it. Just let it flow. Gradually the mantra will fade. The mind will be quiet.*
3. *Occasionally, the quiet will be broken by sporadic thoughts. Let them come. Experience them, then let them leave your mind as quickly as they entered, by simply going stronger to your mantra.*
4. *Keep your movements to a minimum, but if you are uncomfortable, move. Discomfort or anxiety will prevent full attainment of the relaxed state.*
5. *Now practice this method as reflected in steps 2 through 4 for five minutes.*

Here is a simple meditation technique that combines a mantra with visualizations:

1. *Visualize your inner black screen prior to going to sleep, and place one blue speck of light on it. Your eyes are now closed.*
2. *Say out loud the word "OM", or any mantra you have used in the past. Repeat this mantra several times.*
3. *Imagine yourself watching a sunset with someone you care about, or walking in a park or perceive yourself in a weightless body inside your physical body.*
4. *Keep this awareness as you drift off to sleep or keep a constant but vague awareness of your own identity. Then shift your focus from your body into blackness.*

This meditation exercise is designed to train you to experience the depths of your inner being. To do this, you must detach yourself from your normal attachments to thoughts.

This last meditation exercise is one of my favorites and is available on tape through my office:

Focus all of your attention on your breath.

Concentrate on the mechanics of breathing, not the thought of the breath. Note how it comes and goes. As the breath enters and leaves the nostrils, feel the expansion and contraction of the lungs.

Focus on the awareness of breathing. Remove all other thoughts and feelings from your awareness. Observe this natural life process. Do not try to change it. Merely be with it. Let yourself receive the changing sensations that accompany this process.

As you inhale and exhale, one breath at a time, let it happen by itself. If it is deep, let it be deep. If it is slow, let it be slow. If it is shallow, let it be shallow.

If you sense the mind is interfering with this process, just focus on the inhalation and exhalation. Be one with your breath. Nothing else matters.

Observe the uniqueness of each breath. Observe, don't analyze. Note the changing sensations. Be one with your breath.

Ignore all other functions of the body. Remove all thoughts from your mind. You are the breath. Be one with your breath.

You are now floating with the universe. As the wind carries a feather, you are being carried by your breath.

Notice how the distracting thoughts fade. How they become meaningless. All that matters is that you breathe. You are your breath. Be one with your breath.

Let go of the body. Feel as if you have no body. You are weightless, as is your breath.

You are floating in the universe. You are at peace with the universe. You are one with the universe.

Notice how relaxed you are, now that you are free of the confines of the body. You are totally one with the universe.

There is nowhere to go. Nobody is expecting you. You have no schedule or deadline. You are free. Enjoy this moment, for you are one with the universe.

Be quiet. Do not cough or make any movement or sound. Just be still and merge with the universe. You are consciousness.

Let go of all fear and doubt. Let go of all thoughts. Do not try to control your being. Just be free and one with your consciousness.

You have no body. You have no limitations. You are one with your consciousness. You are one with the universe.

Let each moment occur by itself. Observe it and enjoy these intervals of time. Do not resist this merging with your consciousness.

You are now nothing but consciousness. You are the universe.

PLAY NEW AGE MUSIC FOR 15 MINUTES

Now it is time to return to your body. Again, concentrate on your breath. Now note the other functions of your body. Slowly open up your eyes and do what you feel is important at this time.

STRESS

Stress is a matter of interpretation. What is stressful to one person may be neutral to another. How do we know if we are under stress? Consider these twenty-two signs of stress. If you possess seven or more of these you are most likely overstressed:

1. Frequent nervous eye blinking
2. Excessive smoking
3. Easily irritated
4. A lack of sense of humor
5. Digestive problems
6. Regular sensations of tenseness
7. Insomnia
8. Too much sleep (hypersomnia)
9. Cold hands
10. Nervous habits such as frequent tapping of fingers
11. High blood pressure
12. Clenching your jaws and grinding your teeth
13. Shallow and irregular breathing
14. Frequent tension headaches
15. Feelings of inadequacy
16. Excessive use of tranquilizers or antidepressants
17. Excessive drinking
18. Hyperactivity, such as moving your legs back and forth rapidly when seated.
19. Extreme increase or decrease in appetite
20. Loss of interest in sex
21. Clouded thoughts and difficulty in thinking
22. Obsessive thoughts and compulsive behavior

The methods presented in this chapter will assist you in dealing with stress. Here are some additional approaches you will find helpful in overcoming stress:

1. Establish a priority for your daily activities. Keep an activity list and complete tasks in order of importance.
2. Always be yourself. Do not try to please everyone.
3. Develop a realistic attitude towards accomplishing goals. Some things may have to wait until the next day.
4. Select restful hobbies and physical activities to relax. Using competitive sports constantly only adds to your stress.
5. Be optimistic at all times.
6. Master relaxation exercises.
7. Eliminate the tendency to be a perfectionist. Nobody is perfect, notice that all pencils contain erasers.
8. Be assertive and confront people who upset you. Don't accumulate hurt feelings.
9. Learn from your mistakes, but don't dwell on them.
10. When you take a vacation make it purely for relaxation. Don't take working vacations.
11. Incorporate breaks in your day and practice relaxation exercises.
12. Discuss your problems, anxieties and fears with close friends or family.
13. Use low-key exercises to work off tension and frustration.
14. Refrain from insisting you're always right.
15. Eliminate the tendency to second guess your decisions or actions. Life is a numbers game and you can't win them all.

Always deal with the basic cause of stress, rather than with the symptoms. People under stress tend to under-eat or overeat. The latter brings on overweight, sometimes obesity. Extra pounds are an added stress.

BUILDING UP YOUR SELF-IMAGE

Now that we have discussed mind-body techniques and how to deal with stress, the next step is to build up your self-image. By changing any negative attitudes and lowered self-confidence levels to a positive one, you will eliminate the tendency to become discouraged or depressed about losing weight. This will only function to insure your ultimate success.

No amount of will power can surmount this feeling of defeatism. You absolutely must develop feelings of self-esteem and confidence. Think of cultivating a feeling that you will be successful in losing weight permanently and naturally as you would develop a sense that you could accomplish any task you undertook. To initiate this process you need to develop a positive self-image.

Most dieters program negative thoughts into their subconscious daily. They say to themselves or others, "I just can't seem to lose weight," or "I guess I will be fat all of my life." These assertions most likely originate from past failures in attempts to lose weight. However, the constant repetition of these negative statements functions to increase your sense of futility. They represent the opposite of affirmations previously discussed.

All of these negative opinions filter into your subconscious mind, which does not question or analyze the data it receives. The image you have of yourself determines to a large degree how you go about solving problems. If you have experienced repeated failure in past attempts to lose weight, your total image of yourself becomes established and fixed as a failure and permanent "fat" person.

You now become so convinced that you are incapable of reversing this trend that you eventually stop mentally picturing a desirable body image for yourself. Since it is too depressing and frustrating to view yourself as reaching and maintaining your ideal weight, you resign yourself to your overweight and unattractive appearance and indulge in rationalizations (defense mechanisms) to justify this image.

A positive self-image must be fed into your subconscious mind without being evaluated by the critical factor of your conscious mind (defense mechanisms). The most efficient and effective method of accomplishing this goal is by practicing self-hypnosis. We will thoroughly discuss this approach in the next chapter.

Many obstacles may arise during your reducing program, but the proper use of self-programming will transform these former road blocks into stepping stones of success. Now that you will envision yourself as trim, lean and attractive, former difficulties disappear and your subconscious becomes your chief ally in strengthening your ability to meet challenges.

The subconscious mind contains all of our memories. It is our natural computer and is continually being programmed with data originating from the conscious mind (defense mechanisms). The subconscious cannot alter this data. It does, however, direct the conscious mind to act in a certain way. The conscious mind is always resistant to change, any change, even if it is for the better. The conscious mind likes "business as usual." Losing weight is not business as usual, therefore the conscious mind is our only enemy.

A brief example of how the conscious mind acts to keep an overweight person just the way he or she is can be illustrated by watching television. Television is a medium during which many people automatically engage in automatic snacking. Refer back to the section on mindfulness for a complete description of this behavioral pattern.

While watching a certain program let us assume the individual habitually reaches for a bag of potato chips. By the time the program is over, this person has consumed the entire bag. Remember the commercial, "bet you can't eat just one." He or she is completely unaware of the details of this act because these functions were taken over by a poorly programmed subconscious mind.

Consciously, this individual is only thinking of the entertainment from the program. The subconscious now executes this negative behavior pattern through repeated episodes of eating potato chips while relaxing and watching television. It simply follows the orders it has received and stored into its memory banks. Using will power results in ultimate failure because the subconscious programming is unaltered.

By mentally seeing yourself as you desire to be, you are reprogramming your subconscious computer. This does not require a critical acceptance, as your subconscious is incapable of analytical thought. Accompanying this visualization will be a feeling that you have already attained this goal. This "as if" approach is remarkably successful.

Once you achieve your ideal weight using your subconscious mind, the maintenance of this weight will now be effortless. When something attempts to interfere with the proper functioning of the now reprogrammed subconscious, your internal computer will recognize the error immediately and it will be corrected by this feedback mechanism.

Your initial efforts in reprogramming your subconscious will require a certain amount of mental mind set, which encompasses all your new goals and aspirations. Daily practice of the exercises presented in this book will result in a permanent reprogramming of your subconscious computer and a spontaneous incorporation of this goal. Will power is neither necessary nor desirable for this paradigm.

Your imagination must create a new mental image of yourself. If you have properly implanted your subconscious with positive images and suggestions, you automatically alter your behavior to act in accordance with this new programming. A new sense of well-being and accomplishment will accompany this pattern of behavior. You will be able to feel this sense of confidence and psychic empowerment for prolonged periods following additional practice sessions and playing of the tapes recommended.

Will power alone cannot result in permanent weight loss. If it could you would not be reading this book. The problem with will power approaches is that you are consciously placing too much emphasis on past failures. As a result, your mental mind set is not conducive to improvement and subsequent efforts prove only more frustrating.

Success in applying visualization techniques depends upon your subconscious mind's uncritical acceptance of constructive suggestions. The best method of achieving this will be by the use of self-hypnosis. We will fully explore this natural and wonderful technique in the next chapter.

CHAPTER 7

HYPNOSIS—THE ULTIMATE WEIGHT LOSS

TECHNIQUE

Poor eating habits are conditioned and become ingrained in our behavior unless we remove them. These compulsive and involuntary habits have become established through a learning process.

Our conscious mind, or defense mechanisms, represent the critical component of our nature that automatically resists change. Many refer to this as the will power. Self-hypnosis is a natural method that by-passes the conscious mind and directly reprograms the subconscious computer, which stores all of our behavior patterns.

Past attempts to change poor eating habits failed because they required a constant conscious effort. Once a crisis (an emotional problem, for example) distracts the conscious mind, the former dysfunctional eating pattern emerges, since the conscious mind can only deal with one thing at a time under duress.

Through the proper use of self-hypnosis, we can unlearn old patterns and learn new and healthier ways of eating. This approach will also train you to handle all the tensions and frustrations of daily life, without resorting to fattening foods. All you need is the proper motivation to accomplish this goal.

Hypnosis is a natural state of mind that we exhibit approximately seven hours each day. The three hours that we dream at night (the REM cycle) and all of the daydreams that occupy our waking life (reading, watching television, driving, listening to music, etc.) comprise these seven hours. This adds up to 2500 every year!

By using hypnosis we enlist the aid of the part of our mind that contains none of the blocks characteristic of the ordinary waking state, or conscious mind. Hypnosis is a state of mind associated with heightened suggestibility in which we can uncritically accept ideas for self-improvement and then act on them. Hypnosis is *not* brainwashing.

We can express hypnosis by the following equation:

Misdirected attention + belief + expectation = hypnosis

Hypnosis is not sleep, nor is it at any time an unconscious state. When we dream at night we are actually awake! This brainwave has been labeled as alpha by neurologists. During this alpha level we are actually in a state of super-awareness.

The subconscious mind is our computer that stores trillions of pieces of data, and maintains these memories permanently. It directs our behavior. Throughout the hypnotic state, the individual in trance retains complete possession of their faculties and may reject any suggestion they find unsuitable for any reason. There is no mind control with self-hypnosis. All hypnosis is actually self-hypnosis.

It must be remembered that hypnosis does not weaken the will, is not achieved only by less than intelligent people and it is not a form of mind control. Hypnosis is produced by an effective use of our imagination and beliefs. We develop a conviction that we will enter *into* (not under) hypnosis through proper motivation and expectation. Conviction of hypnosis is hypnosis.

You cannot be hypnotized against your will. All hypnosis, as I have stated, is self-hypnosis. When faith, hope, confidence and expectation are all catalyzed by the imagination, hypnosis is the result. Anyone can be guided into self-hypnosis as long as communication is established and fear eliminated.

In reality, hypnosis is a most pleasant experience during which you are relaxed and acutely aware of everything that is said. The critical and analytical conscious mind is by-passed and suggestions are stored as memories in the subconscious where they eventually, upon several repetitions, become a part of your memory bank that operates automatically to help solve your problems.

Since we are continually being exposed to anxiety-provoking food situations in life, we have been programmed to use food as a way of dealing with this form of tension. The subconscious does not possess the ability to reason. It merely carries out what it has been programmed to do.

The computer functions of the subconscious afford us an ideal opportunity to reprogram it and use its ability to store and integrate information resulting in better eating habits and healthier lifestyles.

You need not concern yourself with your ability to terminate a trance state. Nobody has to shake you to end the four hours of daydreaming that you do daily (driving, watch television, reading, etc.). The only other possibility with a hypnotic trance is falling asleep if you practice this method when you are very tired. If this did occur, you would merely nap until your regular "waking up" mechanism aroused you. The feeling you would experience upon arousal would be identical to that from a nap that had not been preceded by hypnosis.

I use the following script to end a trance:

Alright now. Sleep now and rest. You have done very, very well. Listen very carefully. I'm going to count forward now from 1 to 5. When I reach the count of 5, you will be able to remember everything you experienced and re-experienced. You'll feel very relaxed, refreshed and you'll be able to do whatever you have planned for the rest of the day or evening. You'll feel very positive about what you've just experienced and very motivated about your confidence and ability to play this tape again to experience self-hypnosis. Alright now. 1, very, very deep. 2, you're getting a little bit lighter. 3, you're getting much, much lighter. 4, very, very light. 5, awaken. Wide awake and refreshed.

The power of suggestion can often be made to serve us even with a disguised form of hypnotic trance. We enter into a natural level of hypnosis just before retiring and upon arising. For instance, many persons tell themselves before going to bed, "I shall awaken at seven o'clock tomorrow morning. I am going to awaken at seven." They set the alarm at seven-fifteen, for safety's sake, when it is really necessary that they do not oversleep, but invariably they wake at seven according to the suggestion which they gave themselves. Far more reliable than any alarm is that suggestion. It works just as surely and accurately when we send to our subconscious the suggestion, "I am more satisfied with less food every day . . . I see myself slim, trim, comfortable and popular."

There are six basic steps to self-hypnosis. They may be listed as follows:

1. A proper mind set.
2. By-passing the conscious mind.
3. Physical relaxation.
4. Compounding the relaxation.
5. Visualization and therapeutic suggestions.
6. Wake up suggestions with post-hypnotic suggestions. Post-hypnotic suggestions (PHS) are those instructions that are to be carried out following the termination of the trance.

With this background, try this progressive relaxation self-hypnosis induction:

Assume a comfortable position. I highly recommend lying in a recliner to maximize this method.

With your eyes closed take a deep breath and hold it to the count of 6. (Pause) Let it out slowly and take a second deep breath, this time holding it to the count of 8. (Pause) Let it out slowly once again.

Let all of your muscles go loose and heavy. Just relax to the best of your ability. (Pause) Now while the rest of your body continues to relax, I want you to create tension in your arms and fists by clenching your fists tighter and tighter. Just breathing normally, just clench your fists, and straighten your arms by stretching them in front of you, tighter and tighter. (Pause) Feel the tension in your fists and arms while the rest of your body relaxes. Now let your hands and arms relax completely. Just let go and appreciate the relaxation.

Once again clench your fists and straighten your arms. (Pause) Now let go, let your arms and hands relax, relaxing further and further on their own. Relaxing all over. (Pause) Just picture your hands and arms relaxing more and more. Your whole body relaxing. Now, while the rest of your body relaxes, I want you to point your toes away from your body, thereby tensing your feet and legs. Just pointing your toes away from your body, increasing the tension that way. Notice the tension in your leg muscles and feet, study the tension, (pause) and now do the opposite of tension. Relax. Let your feet and legs relax as completely as possible, appreciate the relaxation. Now the contrast between tension and relaxation in your legs and feet. (Pause) Let the relaxation proceed on its own. Now point your feet towards your face, creating tension that way. Once again notice the tension and study it. (Pause) Relax your feet and legs now. Just continue relaxing your legs further and further, the deeper relaxation spreading throughout your body.

Now let us concentrate our attention on the neck, head and facial areas. While the rest of your body continues to relax on its own, just press your head against the back of the chair. Notice the tension in your neck and the back of your head (pause), and now relax your head and neck. Let go of the tension and relax. Note the relaxation in your neck and back of your head, your whole body relaxing more and more. Now, once again, while the rest of your body relaxes, just press your head against the back of the chair. Once again, feel the tension in your neck and head, notice the contrast between tension and relaxation. (Pause) Now stop the relaxation, let the relaxation continue on its own. Easing up, relaxing more and more all the time, deeper and deeper levels of relaxation all the time. Relaxing more and more automatically. Now let us remove any remaining tension in your facial area. Simply close your eyes tighter and tighter. As you do so, feel the tension created by stretching your forehead muscles. Notice this kind of tension, study it. Now relax your eyes, ease up on the forehead. Just relax completely. Your eyes just closed normally now. Let go more and more all over. (Pause) Study the tension in your forehead. (Pause) And now relax your eyes and forehead, your eyes just closed normally now. Feel the relaxation, you can just let the relaxation flow freely throughout your body. Relaxing now

*automatically as you gain the ability to just let your muscles switch off,
switch off completely.*

*Now to take you even deeper into relaxation, I want you to simply
take in a really deep breath and hold it, concentrate any tiny bit of
remaining tension in your chest area. (Pause) Now breathe out the
tension, exhale completely. Relax, and just breathe normally. Picture a
relaxation feeling flowing throughout your entire body.*

*Once again take in a really deep breath and hold it while the rest
of your body relaxes. Just notice the tension in your chest, (pause) and
now breathe out the tension. Just exhale automatically and feel the ever-
increasing waves of relaxation. Calm and serene and more and more
totally at ease. Picture the whole body gong deeper and deeper into
relaxation.*

Stay in this relaxed state for 5 minutes

*Alright now. You have done very well. Listen very carefully. I'm
going to count forwards now from 1 to 5. When I reach he count of 5
you will be able to remember everything you experienced and re-experienced you'll feel very relaxed refreshed, you'll be able to do whatever you
have planned for the rest of the day or evening. You'll feel very positive
about what you've just experienced and very motivated about your ability to get quicker and deeper with each exposure to self-hypnosis. Alright
now. 1, very, very deep. 2, you're getting a little bit lighter. 3, you're
getting much, much lighter. 4, very, very light. 5, awaken. Wide awake
and refreshed.*

To deepen this level, try this method.

*With your eyes closed, I want you to let all of your muscles go loose
and heavy. (Pause) Loose and comfortably heavy. (Pause) Simply let
yourself relax to the very best of your ability, easing up all over now.
(Pause) Relaxing further and further all the time, I want you to take
note of your breathing, listening only to the sound of my voice now, just
notice that as you exhale, you become more comfortably relaxed. (Pause)
Each time you exhale, your whole body can become more and more
deeply relaxed, calm and serene. Easing up and relaxing, appreciating
the deeper and deeper waves of relaxation. (Pause) Relaxing more and
more comfortably heavy, comfortably warm and heavy. A good relaxed*

feeling as your whole body eases up all over. (Pause) Now, to help you go even deeper into relaxation, even further, I want you to picture yourself standing at the top of a long, long escalator, just watching the steps move down slowly in front of you. (Pause) While you watch the steps move downward, notice that each time you breathe out, each time you exhale, you become automatically more relaxed. More and more deeply relaxed. Relaxing now as you watch the escalator stairs go down, down, down (Pause) As you watch the stairs go down, you go down deeper and deeper into relaxation, further and further. Now, imagine yourself grasping the handrails of the escalator safely and securely, you step on the first stair, (pause) and now you actually go down the escalator. As you go down the escalator, it becomes easier and easier to go more deeply into relaxation. Going deeper and deeper all the time now, as you continue to ride the escalator down further and further. (Pause) A good calm serene feeling as you go still further, (pause) deeper and deeper levels of relaxation automatically. Going with the relaxation freely and gently, just easing up all over more and more, (pause) deeper and deeper levels of calm as you continue to ride the escalator down.

Now, while you continue to picture yourself riding down the escalator, safely and securely, I am going to help you achieve an even deeper calm, a deeper level of relaxation. (Pause) Becoming more and more relaxed each time you breathe out, I am going to count from one to three and on the count of three I want you to simply let your muscles switch off completely, thereby doubling your present state of relaxation. (Pause) One, (pause) two, (pause) and three. Doubly down now, doubly relaxed down even further now and further. (Pause) It's easier and easier to become more and more fully relaxed, calm and serene, more and more totally at ease. A good, comfortable heavy feeling as you go all the way down now, all the way, a good comfortably warm, relaxed feeling.

Alright now. You have done very well. Listen very carefully. I'm going to count forwards now from 1 to 5. When I reach the count of 5 you will be able to remember everything you experienced and re-experienced you'll feel very relaxed refreshed, you'll be able to do whatever you have planned for the rest of the day or evening. You'll feel very positive about what you've just experienced and very motivated about your con-

fidence and ability to get quicker and deeper with each exposure to self-hypnosis. Alright now. 1, very, very deep. 2, you're getting a little bit lighter. 3, you're getting much, much lighter. 4, very, very light. 5, awaken. Wide awake and refreshed.

As with all of the hypnotic exercises presented in this book, I suggest you make tapes of the scripts. My book, *New Age Hypnosis* shows you how to do this step by step. If you would like professionally recorded tapes by me, simply contact my office for a comprehensive list of available titles. At the end of this chapter I will present a recommended list of tapes for weight reduction and empowerment.

FORMULATING SUGGESTIONS

I will present several scripts for using self-hypnosis to permanently eliminate improper eating habits and anxiety. These scripts must be general, since each person has unique reasons for their behavior.

This section will train you how to personalize your suggestions so that they will be most effective in your own personal case. Here are some simple rules:

1. All suggestions should be clear and unambiguous.
2. Formulate what you want to program to your subconscious mind prior to entering into self-hypnosis. This is why I recommend the use of tapes.
3. Keep all suggestions positive. A suggestion such as, "food will taste bad to me", is a negative one and is short-lived, ineffective and easily rejected. A better wording would be, "Foods that are low in fat and will help me to attain and maintain my ideal weight will taste so good and be so satisfying, that I will require less of them."
4. Use simple suggestions.
5. Eliminate the use of words such as "must", "should", etc.
6. Keep your most important suggestions until the end of your script.

7. Allow enough time for your subconscious to carry out these suggestions.
8. It is always best to incorporate an emotion with a suggestion. This makes it easier to accept your programming.
9. If you include a suggestion to terminate the trance, make sure you do not state it prior to the completion of your suggestions.
10. Use permissive rather than authoritative suggestions. Suggestions are more easily accepted than commands.

Now you are ready for some additional self-image building suggestions. Try this script:

An average body weight is very desirable to you. You will now eat a healthy diet in amounts required to maintain an average body weight for your height and frame. You now resolve conflicts directly not through the way your body looks.

You have the inner strength and determination to overcome any past tendencies to manifest any type of eating disorder. You will now project a positive self-image, feel balanced and fulfilled, and view life as a tranquil oneness. This will include your own body image.

You love yourself and believe in yourself. Every day, in every way you are becoming empowered and permanently removing all causes and factors that lead to the previous negative eating habits. You absolutely desire this new state of mind, free of all eating problems and reaching and maintaining your ideal weight and body image. You can create your own positive new reality.

Now practice this script for the elimination of guilt and worry:

You are at peace with yourself and your past. You forgive yourself. You learn from the past and you release it. Every day, you feel better and better, all over, in every way.

You are positive and your life becomes positive.

You now see problems only as opportunities. You become positive and optimistic.

You now develop clarity about your desires and goals. You evaluate the potentials and decide what you want. You now have the courage to make life-changing decisions.

You now let go of all fears. You are self-assured and confident about your future. You draw joyous experiences into your life.

You create a happy, successful new reality. You are self-confident and self-reliant. You are worthy and deserving. You let go of the past, are responsible to the present, and create a positive new future.

You create a positive new life. From this moment on, you feel good about your life. You create your own reality, and you create a beautiful life. You release yourself.

You are confident and secure. You retain a calm, optimistic outlook. You feel powerful and in control. Your mind is calm and you think positive thoughts. You now accept the things you cannot change, and change the things you can.

You release your fears, and manifest your desires. You deserve love, prosperity and happiness. You mentally, emotionally and spiritually detach from all forms of negativity and negative people. From this moment on you will project a positive, loving, self-confident and empowered self-image that will permanently eliminate any previous guilt and worry from your awareness.

TRIGGER ZONES

Before I present a detailed script for weight reduction, let us discuss situations to which you react by eating. I refer to these as "trigger zones." The best way to understand this is to write down and enumerate every situation that you associate with habitual, compulsive or emotional eating. I am not referring to physiological hunger, just psychological stimuli to eat.

Some common examples of trigger zones are:

1. When very busy—grabbing a quick snack on the run.
2. Confronted by food situations—preparing foods, supermarket shopping, seeing and smelling tasty fattening foods.
3. Relaxing—watching television, entertaining company at home, coming home from work or school.

4. During routine activities—reading the paper, housework, driving, bookkeeping.
5. Away from home—eating in restaurants, cocktail parties, visiting friends or relatives.
6. Mood swings—boredom, worrying, during or following a crisis, as a "tranquilizer," at the end of a trying day, upon being frustrated by discovering you haven't lost weight.

The next step is to design a healthy resolution to each trigger zone and prepare specific suggestions to resolve that issue. Finding something more constructive and of a positive nature that you can do instead of eating improper foods is your goal with this exercise.

Bear in mind that you will not be able to resolve all these issues at once, but constant repetition will eventually result in a conditioned response which will obviate your need to continually recall them to mind daily.

Now try this rather comprehensive script before we move on to visualization exercises:

Being overweight is unhealthy.

You need your body to live.

You owe your body this respect and protection.

You have the power to reprogram your subconscious mind to reverse the prior thoughts of overeating and thinking of yourself as being overweight. You will, starting today, reprogram your subconscious to think of yourself as being thin and eating only the foods that are healthy and necessary for your body.

You are going to lose all the weight that you desire to lose, and you are going to do this starting today. I want you to associate this relaxed state that you are now in with a relaxed attitude about losing weight. Don't count calories. As you lose weight you will gain more confidence and find further weight reduction easier. When you eat you will cut your food into small pieces and chew them slowly and completely before swallowing. Eat only one mouthful of food at a time. You will find that by eating slowly and smaller portions, you will enjoy your meals better and eat less food. You will find that half way through a meal you will feel full. When this happens you will stop eating. You will never, ever eat when you are not hungry.

Repeat these statements to yourself:

1. *I will get more filling satisfaction from less food every day.*
2. *I will eat slowly and only at mealtimes . . . sparingly and properly.*
3. *I am losing weight steadily every week.*
4. *I am becoming slim and shapely.*
5. *I have a stronger feeling every day that I am in complete control of my eating habits.*
6. *I am developing a greater liking every day for the foods that make me slim and shapely.*

Remember, if you repeatedly deny satisfaction to a hunger pang, the desire eventually goes away.

From this moment on you will not think of yourself as being overweight. Every time such a thought comes into your mind, it programs your subconscious negatively. So you will now monitor your thoughts. Any thoughts or actions which come to your mind about your being overweight will be canceled out by your saying to yourself, "I am thin. I am thin." From this moment on you are only going to eat those foods that are necessary to keep you healthy and mentally alert. You are going to eat smaller portions of the foods necessary to keep you mentally alert and healthy. You will desire no more.

You will be totally aware of eating . . . no longer eat by habit. From this moment on you will no longer eat between meals, or while watching T.V., and you will have absolutely no desire to eat between meals or while watching T.V.

You are going to set a realistic goal for your excess weight loss and you will carry it out successfully. Decide how many pounds you can realistically lose every week and you will lose this exact amount. Now repeat to yourself the realistic amount of weight that you can lose each week until you reach your ideal weight of _____ pounds.

You will find it easier and easier every day to stick to a reducing diet. You will enjoy smaller meals. The irritation and annoyances of everyday life are rolling off you like water off a duck's back. You will thoroughly enjoy the foods that are good for you and healthy also.

Some people fear being thin. But you don't have to fear losing weight. No matter why you gained the weight, for whatever reasons you became a compulsive eater, it is no longer important. What is important is that you have decided to change your eating habits, so that you can reach your desired goal—the image, shape, weight and size that you desire. It doesn't really come into account whether you are fat or become thin. You are still the same person. You still have the same power, the same personality, the same inner reality—no matter what your body shape, weight or size is. There is no need to fear losing any of your self when you lose weight. As the weight and inches roll off, as you control your eating habits, you remain the same you, only more trim. You do not need to fear that you are losing any of your protection. You are the same person.

Don't wait till you lose all the weight to become the person you want to be, if you want to be someone different. Wear the clothes now that project your image. Sit, walk, act with your thin personality. Don't worry about hiding the fat. Wearing fat clothes doesn't hide the fat. They only make you feel worse. So wear the clothes that you want to wear, that project the real you, now, as you are losing weight. This will reinforce your desire to reach your goal.

As that extra weight begins to roll off, to melt away, to disappear, you are totally comfortable with your emerging slender and shapely body. You are perfectly contented and at ease with the emerging slim, trim and slender you. You are in control of your eating habits. You are in control of your life. You are in control of losing weight and you are in control of your personality and your body. And you are perfectly happy with the inner you that remains as you lose weight and inches.

I truly believe that you are capable of dieting successfully and effortlessly to achieve and maintain your ideal weight of _____ pounds. You will be guided by the natural powers within you to achieve and maintain this healthy and attractive body.

Whenever you are tempted to eat fattening food or to violate any of these suggestions, you will automatically ask yourself if you really want to indulge. If you do you will, but you will find that you will prefer to exercise the hypnotic techniques and suggestions that I have given you to reach and maintain your ideal weight.

VISUAL IMAGERY

Human behavior and personality definitely can be made what we wish it to be, depending upon the image we hold of them. The degree of success which we attain depends upon the degree of faithfulness to our imagery, which we exercise. If one day we vision ourselves as slender, for example, and the next day go around complaining about "this awful fat" and "how terrible I look," we accomplish nothing. If we stand before the mirror, and grieve because we are not attractive, we are not holding the image that would make us attractive. Instead, we should refuse to see ourselves as unattractive, but cultivate a pleasing vision, and hold to it as representing ourselves. This is best accomplished by means of self-hypnosis as well as by hypnotherapy.

Research in biofeedback, hypnosis, and meditative states has demonstrated a remarkable range of human self-regulatory capacities. Focused imagery in a relaxed state of mind seems to be the common factor among these approaches.

Imagery of various types has been shown to affect heart rate, blood pressure, respiratory patterns, oxygen consumption, carbon dioxide elimination, brain wave rhythms and patterns, electrical characteristics of the skin, local blood flow and temperature, gastrointestinal motility and secretions, sexual arousal, levels of various hormones and neurotransmitters in the blood, and immune system function. But the healing potentials of imagery go far beyond simple effects on physiology.

Imagery can be an effective tool for helping you to see what changes need to be made, and how you can go about making them. Imagery is the interface language between body and mind. It can help you understand the needs that may be represented by desires to overeat and can help you develop healthy ways to meet those needs.

The two sides of the human brain think in very different ways and are simultaneously capable of independent thought. In a real sense, we each have two brains. One thinks as we are accustomed to thinking, with words and logic. The other, however, thinks in terms of images and feelings.

In most right-handed people, the left brain is primarily responsible for speaking, writing, and understanding language; it thinks logically and analytically, and identifies itself by the name of the person to whom it belongs. The right brain, in contrast, thinks in pictures, sounds, spatial relationships, and feelings. It is relatively silent, though highly intelligent. The left brain analyzes, taking things apart, while the right brain synthesizes, putting pieces together. The left is a better logical thinker, the right is more attuned to emotions. The left is more concerned with the outer world of culture, agreements, business, and time, while the right is more concerned with the inner world of perception, physiology, form, and emotion.

The essential difference between the two brains is in the way each processes information. The left brain processes information sequentially, while the right brain processes it simultaneously. The opposite is true for left handed people.

This ability of the right hemisphere to grasp the larger context of events is one of the specialized functions that make it invaluable to us in losing weight. The imagery it produces often lets you see the "big picture" and experience the way an eating problem is related to events and feelings you might not have considered important. You can see not only the single piece, but the way it's connected to the whole. This change of perspective may allow you to put ideas together in new ways to produce new solutions to old problems. A right-brain point of view may reveal the opportunity hidden in what seems to be a problem. I refer to this as global assessment.

Through imagery, you can learn to relax and be more comfortable in any situation. You can use imagery to help you tap inner strengths and find hope, courage, patience, perseverance, love, and other qualities that can help you eliminate the cause of overeating.

Conditions, such as anxiety, that are caused by or aggravated by stress often respond very well to imagery techniques. The emotional aspects of any habit can often be helped through imagery, and relieving the emotional distress may in turn encourage you to become more empowered and permanently resolve this issue.

Relaxation techniques are the first step in learning to use your images, thoughts, and feelings skillfully. The ability to quiet your mind and concentrate your attention will enable you to make the best use of any technique. You will find that self-hypnosis is by far the most efficient method in attaining a relaxed state.

Learning to relax is fundamental to self-healing and a prerequisite for using imagery effectively. Relaxation is a first exercise in focusing and concentrating your mind on the process of healing. In addition, deep physiologic relaxation has health benefits of its own. It allows your body to channel its energy into repair and restoration and provides respite from habitual patterns of tension.

Active imagery communicates your conscious intentions (or requests) to your subconscious mind. It is a simple process which consists of imagining your desired goal as if it is already achieved while maintaining a passive, relaxed state of mind.

Frequency of practice seems to be a particularly important factor in effectiveness. People who practice their imagery most frequently and enthusiastically receive the most benefit. So when you begin to use imagery, use it often, and use it wholeheartedly. You may think of imagery as an affirmation, a suggestion that will begin to lead you in the direction you desire. Even if you don't feel relief happening right away, be patient and consistent as you imagine the process as vividly as you can.

There are many techniques you may select from for your visualizations. One of the most commonly used is a television screen. By creating your own mental TV show, you are in complete control of the content. A simple change of the station allows you to alter the show. You can relax deeper and deeper as you continue to enjoy your program. Additional deepening, relaxation, and treatment suggestions can be interspersed at this time.

Another popular and successful approach is what I refer to a the sanctuary method. Most people can relate to a pleasant or favorite place. This can be someplace you have been or somewhere you might like to go. Let yourself enjoy your favorite place just as much as you would like. For example, some people think of a time when they went to the beach or ocean. They can almost hear the waves coming in, feel the warmth of the sun, feel the gentle breeze, smell the salty air, etc. As you really enjoy your image, let yourself relax deeper and deeper. Therapeutic suggestions can be made as you continue to enjoy this favorite place.

Here is a script that uses visual imagery via the sanctuary to assist in the reduction of anxiety:

You now have the ability to learn to remain CALM, PEACEFUL, TRANQUIL AND RELAXED through the power of your mind . . . and it is ultimately your mind that will allow you to reach and maintain your ideal weight by eliminating your previous anxiety responses to the world around you. You will find that the words CALM, PEACEFUL, TRANQUIL and RELAXED will help your mind and body to unwind and become calm . . . you will develop a feeling of being tension free whenever you say these four words, CALM, PEACEFUL, TRANQUIL and RELAXED.

Now, I want you to think of a place where you find mental peace and quiet . . . it may be a place with trees . . . mountains . . . water . . . it may be a meadow . . . a lake . . . a stream . . . the ocean . . . and it may be the summer, spring, winter or fall. Notice the smallest details of this sanctuary . . . the colors and textures . . . or perhaps you can hear the sound and smell the scents that you associate with this place . . . or perhaps you can feel the calm, peace, tranquility and relaxation that you associate with this place. Now as your conscious mind becomes more and more involved with your quiet place . . . allow your subconscious mind to help you to maximize this feeling of complete relaxation. Do this now.

PLAY NEW AGE MUSIC FOR 3 MINUTES

Anytime you have any feelings of apprehension all you have to do is to take a deep breath and when you exhale say to yourself CALM . . .

PEACEFUL . . . TRANQUIL . . . RELAXED . . . you will feel your mood change as a feeling of inner calm comes to your body . . .

If you should experience any apprehension or anxiety whatsoever, take a deep breath and when you exhale say the words CALM . . . PEACEFUL . . . TRANQUIL . . . RELAXED . . . you allow yourself to float . . . you enter a state of mind where nothing will disturb you . . .

Here is another sanctuary script:

1. *Visualize yourself in your favorite relaxing environment. This may be the beach, a park or a cabin in the woods. Add to this sounds of nature and the time of the year that you enjoy most.*
2. *Imagine yourself walking along in your favorite environment while looking up at the sky. You notice a rainbow has appeared and you focus your attention on the colors. You seed red, yellow, blue, green, orange, purple and violet.*
3. *As you stare at this rainbow, you realize that as long as you can see it you can accomplish anything you want to do. It is not necessary for this rainbow to be present for you to accomplish your goal, but its presence assures a successful attainment of any quest.*
4. *Sit down now and think of the kind of person you would like to become, a person completely free from guilt and worry. Review personality traits, health issues, finances, and relationships. Focus on specific goals and aspects of your personality. Look up again and note the rainbow. You are now able to accomplish this goal of becoming who you want to be. All of your guilt and worries have now disappeared.*

This next exercise uses visual imagery to assist you in perceiving your ideal body image, free of weight problems.

Mentally see an image of yourself standing before you. This is your body exactly as you would like it to appear, free of any and all negative eating behavior. Look at it more and more closely now, and it will be a realistic but ideal body image, one that you really could achieve, and one that you will achieve. And when you have a very clear image of your body as you would like to have it, keep observing that image, and make it a part of your own reality.

PLAY NEW AGE MUSIC FOR 2 MINUTES

That ideal body image is becoming more and more real, you are seeing it very clearly, and seeing it in its full size and dimensions, and now you are going to step forward and into that body, you will find yourself in that body, so that you can try it out and make certain that it is just the body you do want to have, and if there is something you would like to change, then make those changes now. See yourself free of all desires to overeat. Picture yourself at your ideal weight.

Move around in that body, feel its strength and agility, its dynamic aliveness, its surging vitality, and make really certain that its appearance and all of its attributes are what you realistically desire. And, as you occupy that body, coming to know that body very well, your present physical body is going to be drawn into that new mold. You are moving already towards the realization of that ideal body image, and you will be doing whatever is needed to achieve that body you want to have. You are completely free of all negative eating tendencies.

PLAY NEW AGE USIC FOR 4 MINUTES

Alright now. Sleep now and rest. You did very, very well. Listen very carefully. I'm going to count forward now from 1 to 5. When I reach the count of 5, you will be able to remember everything you experienced and re-experienced. You'll feel very relaxed, refreshed and you'll be able to do whatever you have planned for the rest of the day or evening. You'll feel very positive about what you've just experienced and very motivated about your confidence and ability to play this tape again to experience self-hypnosis. Alright now. 1, very, very deep. 2, you're getting a little bit lighter. 3, you're getting much, much lighter. 4, very, very light. 5, awaken. Wide awake and refreshed.

This visual imagery script will further enhance your subconscious programming to attain your ideal weight:

Imagine yourself at your ideal weight. See a friend/mate shopping with you. Your friend is amazed at your thin appearance. Now visualize two tables in front of you. One table on the right has all the foods you like that add unwanted weight. List examples of these foods. Now draw a large red

"X" through the table and imagine yourself looking at yourself in a side-show mirror (one that makes you look very wide and short).

The table on the left contains food that is healthy and will not add unwanted weight—fish, tuna, eggs, and lean meat, for example. Now draw a large yellow check mark through the table and imagine looking at yourself in a mirror that makes you appear tall and thin. Mentally tell yourself that you desire only foods on the check-marked table. Imagine your friends, family, and parents telling you how great you look by (specify a date), weighing only (specify an amount).

Visualize a photograph of yourself at your ideal weight. Visualize a photograph of yourself at your present weight. Now focus on the photograph of yourself at your ideal weight. The other photograph disappears. Imagine how it will feel at your ideal weight, to bend over to tie your shoelace, walk, jog, or wear a bathing suit on the beach.

Now, mentally select an ideal diet that will help you reach your ideal weight. Tell yourself that this is all the food your body will need or desire and it will not send hunger pangs for more.

When you regularly incorporate mental pictures into your self-hypnosis regimen, you will begin to notice success in your behavioral changes and positive attitude. In my Los Angeles office I work with many celebrities and highly successful corporate executives. One common trait I find among these patients is that *all* of them have imagined themselves attaining success *prior* to them realizing their goals.

The proper and repeated use of "mental movies" will eventually eliminate your old negative self-image and replace it with one that embraces everything you desire. You must reinforce these imageries by actual practice in your daily life, but visualization is the first step to reaching and maintaining your ideal weight permanently and naturally.

It is essential that you have a clear mental picture of how you wish to look and proper eating patterns. Keep this image uppermost in your mind from the beginning of your use of self-hypnosis until your subconscious is reprogrammed.

Another helpful hint in using self-hypnosis is to give yourself suggestions to obtain a deeper and more relaxing trance with each succeeding practice session. You can also implant the thought that your new ideal image will become more clear and attainable.

An increased feeling of confidence will be observed by both yourself and others as you practice with these scripts and tapes. This higher self-image is a sign that you are successfully reprogramming your subconscious. By imagining something long enough and hard enough, it will tend to become a reality, your new positive reality.

Visual imagery approaches work well in removing past trigger zones. For example, let's assume that every Friday evening you and a friend to go out to a restaurant. In the past you may have dieted all week in preparation for this event, and during this meal you probably ordered everything on the menu.

One way to change this pattern is to use mental movies to see yourself at the restaurant eating smaller portions of the proper foods, eating slowly and enjoying the taste more and finally rejecting the previous temptation for second helpings or fattening deserts.

Your new reprogrammed subconscious mind represents a permanent behavioral change. It is now easy to apply this technique to any situation that represented a temptation or trigger zone associated with former dysfunctional eating behaviors.

This approach may be applied each time you are exposed to a trigger zone, or in any way feel that you might be tempted to deviate from your proper eating habits and positive self-image. Since you are not depending on will power or diets, you will find this much more effective than anything you have tried in the past.

It is through the proper use of imagination that we can all take advantage of the many benefits afforded by hypnosis. This is why children between the ages of eight and eighteen make the best hypnotic subjects. Will power has absolutely nothing to do with hypnosis.

Some people think the use of positive thinking of self-hypnosis will be just as effective. Positive thinking only utilizes the conscious mind, so it is dependent on will power alone. Whereas in self-hypnosis we are by-passing the will power and directly re-programming the subconscious.

I cannot overemphasize the value and efficiency of using self-hypnosis tapes to speed up this reprogramming process. Since your subconscious mind has been conditioned to act improperly and react in a manner that is detrimental to your weight loss goal, the repetition of suggestions on a tape that requires no conscious effort will be easy to incorporate in your daily schedule and will yield significant results in a short time.

Through self-hypnosis you will create a desire for the proper foods and enjoy these instead of those that contributed to your former weight problem. By reprogramming your subconscious and using visual imagery, you are actually removing the cause of overeating.

Once the attitude towards a habit is changed, the habit is readily overcome. Dieting is totally unnecessary, and undesirable as I explained in chapter 1. Self-hypnosis allows this task to be pleasurable, has no negative consequences and leads to permanent and natural results.

Self-hypnosis does require that we be true to ourselves. If your conviction to initiate a change is weak, the suggestion will be equally weak and ineffective. The subconscious will not accept weak, half-baked or too general suggestions. It accepts only specific and positive ones that are accompanied by a belief and an expectation of success.

SUPERCONSCIOUS MIND TAP

A NEW AGE method that is extraordinarily effective in eliminating weight problems is a technique that I developed in 1977 known as the superconscious mind tap. The basis for this technique is to raise the quality of the subconscious mind's energy.

We have a component of our subconscious that is perfect and is called the superconscious mind or Higher Self. By introducing our subconscious mind to its perfect counterpart (the superconscious) through self-hypnosis, we can effect a raise in the quality of the energy (electromagnetic radiation) that comprises the subconscious. I call this technique "cleansing."

A thorough discussion of cleansing is presented in my book *Soul Healing*.[6] For our purposes, the following script will train you in the art of accessing your Higher Self for the purpose of losing weight permanently and naturally:

Now listen very carefully. I want you to imagine a bright white light coming down from above and entering the top of your head, filling your entire body. See it, feel it and it becomes reality. Now imagine an aura of pure white light emanating from your heart region, again surrounding your entire body, protecting you. See it, feel it and it becomes reality. Now only your Higher Self, masters and guides and highly evolved loving entities who mean you well will be able to influence you during this or any other hypnotic session. You are totally protected by this aura of pure white light.

In a few moments, I am going to count from 1 to 20. As I do so you will feel yourself rising up to the superconscious mind level where you will be able to access your Higher Self and both explore and remove the causes of your overeating. Number 1, rising up. 2, 3, 4, rising higher. 5, 6, 7, letting information flow. 8, 9, 10, you are halfway there. 11, 12, 13, feel yourself rising even higher. 14, 15, 16, almost there. 17, 18, 19, number 20. Now you are there. Take a moment and orient yourself to the superconscious mind level.

PLAY NEW AGE MUSIC FOR 1 MINUTE

You are now in a deep hypnotic trance and from this superconscious mind level, there exists a complete understanding and resolution of the weight problem. You are in complete control and able to access this limitless power of your superconscious mind. I want you to be open and flow with this experience. You are always protected by the white light.

At this time I would like you to ask your Higher Self to explore the origin of your overeating. Trust your Higher Self and your own ability to allow any thoughts, feelings or impressions to come into your subconscious mind concerning this goal. Do this now.

PLAY NEW AGE MUSIC FOR 3 MINUTES

Now I would like you to let go of the situation, regardless of how simple or complicated it may seem. Allow your Higher Self to facilitate the raising of your soul's energy to the level well above having any form of overeating or weight problem.

At this time I want you to see yourself in your current awareness and consciousness free of overeating and visualizing yourself at your ideal weight.

PLAY NEW AGE MUSIC FOR 4 MINUTES

You have done very well. Now I want you to further open up the channels of communications by removing any obstacles and allowing yourself to receive information and experiences that will directly apply to and help better your present awareness. Allow yourself to receive more advanced and more specific information from your Higher Self to raise your soul's energy and remove overeating and weight problems from your awareness. Do this now.

PLAY NEW AGE MUSIC FOR 4 MINUTES

Alright now. Sleep now and rest. You have done very, very well. Listen very carefully. I'm going to count forward now from 1 to 5. When I reach the count of 5, you will be back in your current conscious awareness. You will be able to remember everything you experienced. You'll feel very relaxed, refreshed and you'll be able to do whatever you have planned for the rest of the day or evening. You'll feel very positive about what you've just experienced and very motivated about your confidence and ability to play this tape again to experience your Higher Self. Alright now. 1, very, very, very deep. 2, you're getting a little bit lighter. 3, you're getting much, much lighter. 4, very, very light. 5, awaken. Wide wake and refreshed.

We can summarize the steps in using self-hypnosis for permanent and natural weight loss as follows:

1. Practice self-hypnotic induction techniques. Find one that is comfortable for you and use it daily. For a comprehensive presentation of these techniques I refer you to my book, *New Age Hypnosis*[7]

2. Reprogram your subconscious by direct suggestions to build up your self-image and confidence.
3. Use visual imagery by way of mental movies to establish desired eating habits, and picture yourself at your ideal weight.
4. Utilize posthypnotic suggestions and program yourself to activate the subconscious appropriately whenever you are tempted to revert to prior dysfunctional behavior.
5. Program solutions to your trigger zones and use visualization techniques during your self-hypnosis to facilitate your successful elimination of prior negative responses.
6. Learn from your failures by treating them as new trigger zones and use them to your advantage for continued improvement.
7. Keep using your tapes after initial successes. Do not terminate this training and growth approach prematurely.
8. Use cleansing to raise the quality of your subconscious mind's energy and permanently eliminate the previous weight problem.

If you are looking to self-hypnosis as a magic wand which will instantly help you cure your obesity, you will be disappointed. The same is true of hypnotherapy. As long as you expect *someone else* to do something *to you* to lose weight, you will fail. I have presented to you a definite, specific and detailed method of self-improvement. You must practice to attain this goal, but once you acquire it, you will be very richly rewarded and empowered. At no time have I asked you to use your will power to stop over eating.

The procedures that you are being asked to follow are simple and efficient, but they do require continued daily practice before you can reap the maximum benefits. The results will ultimately become permanent if you do not prematurely discard the program. Eventually, the self-hypnotic conditioning sessions will only take a brief amount of your time.

You will be quite pleased when you discover, as many of my patients have found, that you can go about your daily activities without constantly having to think about your eating habits. You will be grateful for having learned a method which does not require a constant conscious effort. All of this may be facilitated by using self-hypnosis tapes.

One of my patients, whom I shall refer to as Brenda, came to me in June of 1996 to lose 100 pounds. The following May she sent me the following letter, accompanied by two photos illustrating her 50 pound weight loss so far:

May 8, 1997

Dear Dr. Goldberg:

Please feel free to use these photos to help someone else.

My current weight loss is 50 lbs. . . . The "mid-term". Eventually, I'll send you the Final.

Last June, I felt such hopelessness and despair. Today I have inner peace and strength. I look forward to the future and dedicating my life to helping others.

Maybe these pictures can give another person courage, and faith that they can do it, too.

The reactions to these photos from my friends and clients have been:

"Oh my God."

Brenda

RECOMMENDED SELF-HYPNOSIS TAPES

Many of my readers contact my office requesting self-hypnosis tapes recorded by me to assist them with their personal and spiritual growth. My website (www.drbrucegoldberg.com) details over 100 audio cassettes.

You are welcome to contact my office for a complete list of my self-hypnosis tapes if you own a computer. The following tapes are highly recommended:

WEIGHT REDUCTION—Permanently change your eating habits and reach and maintain your ideal weight.

INSOMNIA—Remove sleep disturbances and regularly obtain a night of quality rest.

ANXIETY—Regain the peace and harmony in your life and increase your resistance to stress.

DEPRESSION—Elevate your mood without medication and increase both your energy and enjoyment of life.

SLOWING DOWN THE AGING PROCESS—Retain or regain a youthful vigor and add 25 to 50 quality years to your life.

SUPERCONSCIOUS MIND—Raise the quality of your soul's energy through "cleansing" and access your Higher Self.

THE PERSONAL EMPOWERMENT PROGRAM

A Six Cassette Training Program

a. Eliminate Guilt and Worry—Remove these two useless emotions from your awareness.

b. Positive Thinking and Actions—Eliminate cynical, defeatist and negative thinking as you become a doer and achiever, free of procrastination and attaining goals.

c. Dream Power—Use your nightly REM cycle to solve problems and empower yourself.

d. Overcome Procrastination—Remove, once and for all, the most important block to your personal and professional fulfillment.

e. Increase Your Brain Power—Learn how to maximize your thought processes and vastly increase our knowledge and memory.

f. Assertiveness—Learn how to avoid being manipulated and begin the process of taking charge of your life.

CHAPTER 8

PUTTING IT ALL TOGETHER

Past difficulties with losing weight are due to overeating and improper eating, coupled with a lack of exercise. Obsession with food, despite your best intentions, leads to compulsive eating behavior.

You end up dissatisfied when you eat, dissatisfied when you don't eat and feeling guilty due to this lack of control. The answer to this dilemma is not to be concerned with devising a plan to ensure successful under-eating. Rather, if you can eliminate overeating, eating in excess of your body's natural requirements, you will have solved the problem. The problem is not overweight but overeating.

Health risks of overweight are as much a matter of rapid weight change as of overweight per se. Rapid weight loss is a health hazard, but so is rapid weight gain. Dieting causes overeating. Compulsive eating, a common side effect of dieting, is eating that is out of sync with the body's natural needs; it is eating for all the wrong reasons.

Dieting involves restricting one's intake. This may involve particular classes of food or just overall calories. It may involve severe restrictions, all the way down to protein-supplemented fasts, or just mild deprivations. The dieter learns to give precedence to what the diet allows over what the body demands. Restrictive dieting drives a wedge between a person and his or her body. The dieter has confused and distorted the natural connection between eating and the body's natural signals.

Instead of eating on the basis of natural hunger and satiety cues, the dieter eats on the basis of caloric calculations or abstruse nutrient combinations. Still dieters are prone to mood swings that bring on binges, and for some reason, emotional swings seem to increase in frequency and amplitude when they diet.

This loss of control destroys healthy eating patterns, results in weight gain and undermines self-esteem. For these and many other reasons discussed in this book, never, ever go on a diet again. To cure yourself permanently of weight problems you must make peace with yourself.

Food is not really the problem at all. Food is delicious and nourishing. Your problem is that, you use food to manage your anxiety, to calm yourself when you feel stressed, and to bring comfort when you feel lonely or sad or afraid.

Because you alternate between using food to keep yourself comfortable and desperately trying to limit your intake, you've forgotten the true purpose of eating. For you, food no longer has anything to do with physiological hunger.

It is time to make specific and permanent changes in your behavior. Learn to eat entirely from physiological hunger and stop overeating. Give up relying on diets and move beyond your negative preoccupation with eating and weight into a fuller life. Always bear in mind that we define normal weight as the natural weight you will return to once you cure your compulsive overeating.

It is time to remove all beliefs you accepted about being "fat." You most likely have resigned yourself to labeling your behavior as lacking in discipline and willpower, self-indulgent, greedy, infantile, out of control and weak. Disregard the concept that there is an "ideal" body and that yours is far from it. Eating is not something that needs to be "controlled."

Eating is often as possible in response to physiological hunger is normal and a main component in my recommendations. By following this plan you will find yourself having less need to resort to food when you're anxious. Soon, the needs of your body begin to determine when, what, and how much you eat and you will reestablish your natural weight.

The body always responds to dieting as a threat and slows down its metabolism in order to store fat. This is the exact opposite of what you want to happen. The more you diet, the slower your metabolism, and with each successive diet it becomes more difficult, if not impossible, to lose weight. The ultimate result of food deprivation is an increase in stored fat.

It is time to end this punishment of yourself by restricting your food intake. Consider how ridiculous it is to use dieting (a punishment) to deal with your "out-of-control" behavior. This is masochism and guaranteed to fail.

Eating, overeating, under-eating, any eating, is not a crime, but when you confine yourself by dieting, you are sentencing yourself to a form of diet prison. You are not questioning why you eat or what you can do about it. You are simply saying "Stop."

Diets are fundamentally confinements much like prisons, and dieters, like prisoners, do time for not looking right and not eating right. This analogy is a good one in that all prisoners share a common fantasy, rebellion. As convicts dream about receiving the cake with the proverbial file, dieters just dream about the cake.

We cannot be our own warden and prison guard. People never scold themselves into significant change. Change comes about through nurturing support and reprogramming the subconscious. Three simple steps will assist you in developing proper eating habits.

The first step is to catch yourself in the act of thinking negatively about your eating or your weight. Secondly, confront your negative thoughts directly and challenge them with your new awareness about your eating, your weight, and the process of change. What makes it possible to stop your negative thoughts is your conviction that they simply do not work. By making a pact with yourself that each time a negative thought reasserts itself, you will put it aside and replace it with a nonjudgmental view, you are laying a firm foundation for the last step.

The final step consists of reprogramming your subconscious using any of the several techniques presented in this book. The new positive you will now want to eat right, exercise and live the healthy, empowered life of a quality soul.

We must learn to live in the present and replace negative judgments with self-acceptance. Ninety-eight percent of dieters regain their lost weight and more. Starving yourself only ensures a rebellion by your mind and body known as bingeing. Diets result in weight gain eventually.

The only hunger you need to respond to by eating is physiological hunger, the hunger that sustains life. Psychological hunger is reflected by eating:

"Just because it's there."

"Because it's time for breakfast/lunch/dinner."

"Because you feel lonely/anxious/depressed."

"Because it tastes good."

"Because you feel happy/excited/like celebrating."

In the past you have failed in your attempt to control psychological hunger with either dieting or will power. Occasionally, you may have confused these two different types of hungers and threw this delicate balance off. We each have an internal mechanism that will tell us when your stomach is empty and when it is full. Once you get back in touch with that mechanism, you will be able to respond to it.

If this is the case, then you are going to have to relearn what physiological hunger is and what it feels like. This requires you to eat according to your hunger rather than to the clock. Your new goal is to abandon entirely all external cues like calories charts, mealtimes, or social gatherings so that you can rediscover the internal cues you buried years ago. Your body will direct the process.

I cannot overemphasize the value of eating solely in response to physiological hunger. You will never gain weight as long as you eat properly when these true hunger pangs strike. Not only will you not gain weight, but you will steadily lose weight until your body attains its ideal weight. In our daily lives stress, social responsibilities and other factors tempt us into eating when we are not hungry.

The following eating exercise is only to be practiced if you truly can't differentiate between physiological and psychological hunger. Getting as hungry as often as possible during the day is the goal of this approach.

I suggest you select a day when you feel most in control of your life, one on which you are relatively relaxed. For some people the weekend, away from the stress of work routines, is best. Others are more comfortable approaching this exercise during the week, when work schedules give structure to their time. Whichever day you pick for the experiment, you'll have to give up all routine eating in favor of feeling your body's signals, and you must assure yourself access to an ample supply of food.

Each time you feel hungry eat only a small amount of low-fat and high-fiber food. Limit your quantities to ensure as many hunger experiences as possible. Begin this exercise upon arising. If you truly feel hungry, eat a light recommended meal. After lying in bed for a few minutes, psychological hunger will pass, but not physiological hunger. The absence of hunger pangs should be followed by allowing yourself time to shower, dress, and go about your early morning business. Half an hour later, sit down and give yourself another quiet moment to tune in to your stomach. Are you hungry yet?

Again, if you are hungry enjoy a small meal. It is not the purpose of this exercise to deprive your body of needed nourishment. The lack of hunger pangs should be followed by carrying on with your day by skipping breakfast.

Throughout the morning continue monitoring your stomach. If it is registering hunger pangs eat a small meal. Keep this regimen up throughout the entire day. I recommend at least a ten minute wait following a hunger pang before you eat something.

By the time you retire for the evening, you should have learned what physiological hunger feels like. Take this time to review your day and compare the sensation of physiological hunger to your previous eating associations with psychological hunger. No doubt you will derive greater pleasure from eating as a response to physiologic hunger.

This exercise is valuable in that it tunes you into your body. When you tune in to your body, you are turning over to it the process of weight loss, allowing your body to tell you when, what, and how much to eat. Once you do this, you will begin to return to your natural weight. Eating from physiological hunger alone automatically begins a weight loss process until you reach your ideal weight. This is due to the fact that your excess weight is the result of eating when you aren't hungry or eating foods you aren't hungry for or eating more food than your stomach wants. When you stop that kind of eating, your weight will drop.

Here are a few additional techniques that will assist you in learning to identify when your stomach is full physiologically:

- *When you eat your next regular meal, chew your food slowly. Take at least twenty minutes to finish this meal. Eat until you experience a certain level of satisfaction. Now stop eating and see if additional hunger pangs of the physiological type persist. If they do, continue eating and stop eating if they don't.*
- *Another approach is simply to take a few bites and stop eating. See if you are still hungry. If so, take a few more bites and stop again. Take a walk for a few minutes before continuing, then repeat this procedure (minus the walk) until you feel satisfied.*

Losing weight is just one of the benefits you will experience by following the recommendations in this book. The permanent loss of pounds is a pleasure, a side effect and fringe benefit of the profound alteration in the quality of your life for the better.

Do not think that you will never eat a snack again. I have nothing against snacks, as long as they are in response to physiologic hunger and consist of low-fat foods. Healthy snacking can help maintain a higher level of nutrition and energy than eating larger, less frequent meals. The main problems with this plan are that Americans' most popular snack foods also happen to be among the highest in fat content, and it's easy to lose track of what and how much we actually consume when snacking.

It is difficult for the average person to accept many of the paradigms present in this book. This is to be expected, considering the amount of media brainwashing we are exposed to. There are three types of deprivation we may experience in life. The first is lack of food. This meal skipping will only result in overeating at your next meal.

Lack of sleep constitutes the second type of deprivation. This often is associated with overeating, especially midnight snacking. Boredom is due to a lack of stimulation, and this represents the third way in which deprivation can manifest itself. Many studies show that people who are at their normal weight eat mostly because of physiological hunger. Whereas obese people eat as a result of emotional states, such as anger, depression, excitement, happiness, or boredom.

The common effect of deprivation of any type is overeating. Practicing the exercises presented in this book will place you in complete control of your life and you will not have to worry about being subject to any of these deprivation categories.

Here are some additional tips to change negative eating patterns:

- Allot at least twenty minutes for each meal. It requires about twenty minutes for the brain to receive the message that the stomach is full. Setting a timer will help you cue into your body's sense of hunger.
- Create an atmosphere at home which adds to the pleasure of eating. Use music, colorful place settings, candles, fresh flowers and anything else that brings you pleasure while you dine.
- Brush your teeth if you have a significant psychological hunger pang and don't have low-fat food in your home.
- Keep all of your eating to one place in your home. This will eliminate the automatic eating while watching television or in the den or in the kitchen while on the telephone.

- Be happy with slight weight loss, such as a pound a week. More rapid weight loss is mostly muscle tissue, water and important minerals and nutrients. Patience is a necessity for permanent weight loss.
- Keep your leftovers wrapped in aluminum foil instead of plastic wrap. Overweight people are more stimulated to eat when they can visibly see the food.
- Start dinner with a glass of chilled tomato juice.
- Order fish, seafood, white poultry, egg white omelets, vegetables, fat-free yogurt in restaurants. Remember, white is light and green is lean.

EIGHT SIMPLE WAYS TO LOSE WEIGHT

1. Switch the portions and ratios of food groups at your meals. For instance, double the size of vegetable servings, while cutting in half chicken, fish or meat portions.
2. Skim fat from soups before heating. Drop ice cubes into the soup, or refrigerate, and then lift the fat off the top.
3. Have your meals on small plates.
4. Make a commitment to walk, or bike, all distances under a mile.
5. Plan ahead for high calorie meals. If you're going out to dinner, eat lighter meals during the rest of the day.
6. No matter what high-fat food is on sale, keep to the low-fat, high-volume and high-quality rule when you shop.
7. Rinse canned vegetables for a full minute. You'll cut the salt by 40 percent and reduce your water retention.
8. Eat a strictly vegetarian diet at least four days a week.

Since 1974 I have personally trained several thousand patients to lose weight permanently. There are common traits that are exhibited by these successful patients. Here are some of the characteristics I have observed in patients who have successfully lost weight and positively changed their lives:

1. Positive self-talk. These people continually say nice things to themselves. If they slip in their eating habits, a typical response might be, "I resolve not to repeat this error and be more careful the remainder of the day."
2. They discover what works for them and continue utilizing these methods. Target weight goals set are always realistic.
3. A strong belief in their ability to attain and maintain their ideal weight is exhibited.
4. Successful weight losers enjoy life.
5. These patients exercise regularly.
6. They lost weight for themselves, not someone else.
7. It was not difficult for them to learn and adopt a new way of eating for the rest of their life.
8. They deal with slipups immediately.
9. Those that have kept off excess for many years face and confront their feelings. They get to the source of the negative emotion by noticing the feeling, identifying the cause and figuring out a way to solve the problem.

A FINAL WORD ABOUT FOOD GROUPS

To lose weight both safely and permanently, the main consideration is the amount of vital energy you have at your disposal and the efficiency to use this energy to eliminate waste products from your body. Excess weight in the form of fat comprises some of these wastes. One result of this is a freeing up of energy and an increased feeling of vitality.

We must never forget that our body is self-cleansing, self-maintaining and self-healing. Take the human heart for example. This organ beats 100,000 times every twenty-four hours, pumping six quarts of blood through over 96,000 miles of blood vessels. Over twenty-four trillion cells comprise this six quarts of blood that make between 3,000 to 5,000 trips throughout the body daily. We produce 7,000,000 new blood cells every second!

This perfectly run mechanism is designed to maintain our body temperature 98.6 degrees Fahrenheit. A perfect balance is always maintained, as our digestive system connects the food we eat into healthy tissues and cells. Another astonishing fact is that this system reproduces itself throughout our life, as all of the cells are replaced in our body every nine months.

Over seventy-five trillion cells work in harmony to maintain our vital functions so that we can sustain life. The smallest cell in your body is approximately one billion times the size of its smallest component. The DNA, mitochondria, hormones, enzymes, organelles, amino acids and thousands of other substances work in harmony like a well organized manufacturing plant.

My point in describing the wonders of our body's physiology is to illustrate that this innate system is designed for health, and health also includes being at your ideal weight. As long as we work with nature and consume its food groups properly, this optimal health is our destiny.

One problem we face is toxemia. Our body builds toxemia (a poisoning of the blood) in two ways. The first is through normal metabolic processes, and the second is by the residue resulting from the foods not efficiently utilized. Excess weight results when more of these residues build up. A further complication comes from the fact that these toxins are acidic and the body retains water to neutralize this chemical imbalance. This leaves you feeling bloated and weighing more.

The body is designed to store the fat produced from these toxins away from its vital organs. Such locations as the midsection, under the chin, thighs, buttocks and upper arms are chosen. These most undesirable places aesthetically only add to our lowered self-images, as well as producing feelings of lethargy and general discomfort.

One way to begin to improve our body's metabolism is to refrain from eating and drinking water at the same time. The stomach produces digestive juices to break down food. By drinking water along with your meal, you are effectively diluting these juices. This results in an additional strain placed on the stomach, hinders the efficiency of food metabolism, wastes energy and interferes with the elimination of waste products. Excess weight is the result.

We can help our body immensely by consuming high-water content food that will function to remove toxic waste products efficiently thereby causing weight loss. Fruit has the highest water content of any food in nature; it is composed of between 80 and 90 percent water.

Interestingly enough, our predecessors were predominantly fruit eaters. Hominid teeth studied in the 12,000,000 year period leading up to Homo Erectus demonstrated that these people ate a diet consisting almost entirely of fruit.

Fruit is a cleansing food that, unlike some proteins, will not clog the arteries. We need the least amount of energy to digest fruit as compared to any other food. We don't even digest fruit in the stomach, as it is predigested. Some fruits, such as dried fruit, dates and bananas, stay in the stomach longer. Within thirty minutes all fruits are passed through the stomach to the small intestines. This results in a freeing of extra energy to cleanse the body of toxic waste.

It is best to eat fruit alone and on an empty stomach. It should not be consumed with or immediately following any other food. Fruit is by far the most important food you can eat to lose weight permanently.

PROTEIN

Of all the foods we consume, protein is the most complex and the most difficult to assimilate. Diseases such as ulcers, gout, arthritis, osteoporosis, and cancer of the breasts, liver and bladder have been linked to an over consumption of protein.

Between twenty-five and thirty hours represents the average time for food (except fruit) to move through the gastrointestinal tract. Eating protein in the form of meat more than doubles this time. This results in a drain on our body's energy reserve and an accumulation of toxic waste products, some of which are stored as fat.

We simply do not need as much protein as we have been led to believe. Our body produces about seventy percent of the protein it needs. The recommended daily allowance (RDA) of protein is fifty-six grams (less than two ounces) daily. Most of us consume too much protein, having it at every meal.

We have been brainwashed to think that meat is required for strength. Isn't it interesting that the strongest animals on the planet, elephants, horses, oxen, water buffalo and silverback gorillas, all are herbivores? Steers eat grass and grain and gorillas consume fruit and vegetables. Where do they get their tremendous strength from?

The answer is simple. There are many sources of protein, and no single source is better or worse in building muscle mass, which is the basis of strength. These muscle tissues are built from amino acids, not protein per se. The better we utilize the amino acids in our food, the more efficient we are in producing muscle mass.

Fleshy foods contain no essential amino acids that we cannot obtain from plants. Out of the twenty-three amino acids, fifteen can be produced by our body. That leaves eight that must be derived from our food. Consuming nuts, seeds, fruits and vegetables regularly will provide these eight essential amino acids in abundant quantities.

Some fruits and vegetables contain all eight of these essential amino acids. Examples are bananas, carrots, cabbage, corn, cauliflower, eggplant, peas, tomatoes, brussel sprouts, cucumbers, kale, okra, potatoes, all nuts, beans, peanuts, sunflower seeds and sesame seeds. The utilizable amino acid content in these plant sources are higher than that contained in fleshy animal meat.

There is absolutely no nutritional or physiological justification for us to eat meat. Only carbohydrates supply energy. Meat contains virtually no carbohydrates and provides no fuel for our body. There is practically no fiber content in meat. What meat does contain is saturated fat, the type of fat that causes heart attacks.

Meat also releases uric acid into our blood as it is metabolized. Since we lack the enzyme to break down uric acid (uricase), this substance becomes toxic and damages our body. From this discussion

I trust you see that eating meat has only one effect on our health, it deteriorates it.

For those engaged in athletics, additional protein in the diet does not produce extra strength. What it does do is cause loss of appetite, dehydration and diarrhea. Since it requires far more energy to digest and metabolize protein, a drain on the athlete's energy results. Consider a lion, whose diet is exclusively flesh. This animal sleeps twenty hours a day. Now compare this to an orangutan, which eats only plants. Orangutans sleep only six hours daily. We can prevent over ninety percent of heart disease by eating a vegetarian diet.

Other considerations in relationship to the various food groups that will assist you in permanently losing weight are:

- If you are allergic to dairy products, eat raw nuts for calcium. This is also indicated for women to replenish the drop in calcium experienced at the onset of their menstrual cycle.
- Eat only whole-grain breads.
- Only use seasonings, condiments and dressings that do not contain chemical additives and preservatives like MSG.
- Keep your consumption of garlic and raw onions to a minimum. They cause cravings for high-fat foods.
- Substitute lemon juice for vinegar in salad dressings. This will improve your ability to digest starches.

OVEREATING

The most important theme of this book is to not overeat. We overeat for many psychological reasons, as I have discussed throughout this book. Physiologically we eat too much because our bodies are not absorbing enough nutrients.

Waste products from metabolism clog the tiny villi in our small intestines. These filaments function to absorb nutrients. The body continues to send hunger pangs to the stomach, regardless of how much we have consumed, in order to satisfy its nutrient requirements.

This is especially relevant when we eat junk food and processed foods. Nutritional deficiencies are unfortunately quite common in American teenagers, the largest consumers of junk food. Statistically sixty percent of those individuals, and Americans in general, are overweight.

A malnourished body will demand more and more food. Eating quality foods, and those rich in water content, will facilitate our metabolism, remove toxic waste products, free up more energy and allow us to lose weight permanently and naturally.

CRAVINGS

If you are patient enough to delay satisfying a craving for between four to twelve minutes, most of these urges disappear. Most people crave foods made with sugar, flour and/or fat.

Men love salty, crunchy foods, chips, pretzels, salted nuts. Women and younger people of both sexes love sweets, especially chocolate. Everyone loves finger foods. Creamy foods evoke childhood. They're often high in fat, which has a slightly sedating effect. Puddings, mashed potatoes and ice cream are examples of this category.

A WRITTEN PLAN TO LOSE WEIGHT PERMANENTLY

To initiate a permanent change in your life is to make a commitment. What better way to formalize this goal than with a written plan. This keeps your intentions clear and adds a certain reality to your goal. Think of it as a contract with yourself. Another way to look at it is a way to help you keep your goals in mind, monitor your progress, and evaluate what is and isn't working.

The first step in this plan is to write down your goals. This includes self-image improvements, weight loss, exercise regimens and any other lifestyle changes you desire. Always be specific and state exactly what you'll do, how often, when, and how you will know you have successfully achieved your goal.

Next, divide your goals into smaller sub-goals that contain clear and do-able steps. Don't demand of yourself more than you can handle. Build in some flexibility, so that you are less likely to abandon this plan. Always make sure your goals and sub-goals are realistic.

Thirdly, apply what is known as the confidence test. If you can honestly say to yourself that you are at least 70 percent certain that you can accomplish your proposed goal within your planned time frame, it is do-able. Lower your goal if your confidence level is less than 70 percent, and raise it if it is higher than 90 percent. Lastly, place your written plan in a location in both your home and office where it will be seen daily. This affords you the opportunity to check on your progress.

Always identify potential problems that may dissuade you from your goals and solve them, avoid them, prepare for them or simply cope with them differently than you did in the past. Keep positive self-talk statements and continually challenge negative thoughts.

Set up a support system by enlisting the aid of family and friends. Announce to the world your intention to change. Share your plans with the people closest to you. By letting others know your intentions, you may help channel peer pressure into support.

One of the themes I have tried to emphasize in this book is that of complete empowerment. This is brought about by mind-body interactions encompassing the physical, mental, emotional and spiritual components of our being.

Mindfulness is an important part of this paradigm. Through mindfulness we become aware of all the choices we have and act accordingly on these options. It involves a realization that we don't have to run our lives on automatic pilot. We can read labels, notice how our food tastes, turn off the television, work on our life goals, relationships and maximize our potential.

We must always remember that we ourselves are primarily responsible for our health. Our emotional and lifestyle choices determine our health and well-being more than anything else. This sense of empowerment results from an improved feeling of self-sufficiency and self-esteem that overshadows any fear.

We accelerate our growth when we can care for ourselves on many different levels. You do not have to be perfect to permanently lose weight. One disadvantage of perfectionism is that it often makes us feel guilty and ashamed and propagates a negative self-image. Compulsive behaviors often result, such as workaholism, alcoholism and compulsive overeating.

I honestly feel that we were born with an innate ability to live a healthy and empowered life. This entails being at our ideal weight throughout life and physically, emotionally, mentally and spiritually healthy.

Instead of empowerment perhaps we should call this a *re-powerment*. Bringing back the power we were born with to take charge of our lives and spread this positivity to all we come in contact with is another theme of this book.

CONCLUSION

All the diets now available in print are bought with anticipation, read with interest, tried with hope and discarded with disillusionment. They all demand sacrifices the average overweight or obese individual is not prepared to make since he feels he can only make these sacrifices for a limited time. As I have emphasized many times throughout this book, diet is a treatment and not a cure for obesity. To attain the latter you must achieve permanent correction of your mistakes, that is, your faulty eating habits.

It is easy to become frustrated following a binge or day during which we may have eaten high-fat and low quality foods. Always bear in mind that it is the amount of fat we eat on average and our overall activity level that makes the difference, not the eating we do at any single meal or lack of activity on any single day. Perfection is not a prerequisite in order to be healthy and lean. As my late grandmother used to say, "It all comes out in the laundry."

Simple strategies will assist you in reaching and maintaining your ideal weight. Identify your emotional trigger zones, and deal with them through mind-body techniques and involvement in nonfattening activities. Secondly, learn to externalize your problems and seek constructive solutions. This requires assertive behavior

I cannot underestimate the value of exercise. There is simply no good excuse for not being involved in *regular* physical activity. People who choose not to make time for physical activity on a *consistent* basis rarely if ever succeed in maintaining their desired best weight.

Physical activity can easily be incorporated into our daily lives. Do not limit yourself to your isolated workouts to engage in exercise. Always seek ways to add physical "labor" to ordinary tasks instead of relying on labor-saving devices. Engage in several different types of activities, such as walking, biking, swimming, or weight training for variety.

Adopt nonfood hobbies such as gardening, bowling or home improvement to occupy your spare time, reduce stress and burn additional calories. Do not forget to exercise formally at least every other day for at least one half hour.

There are many reasons to lose weight. Some people merely want to look better. This may be considered vanity, or simply a desire we feel we owe to ourselves and those who are obliged to look at us.

Being at our proper weight affords us peace of mind, better health and has obvious advantages in our social and business life. Do we not live in a society obsessed with looking good? Even in business we hear the expression "lean and mean."

Reaching and maintaining our ideal weight is more economical. It also fosters a positive self-image, especially to children. Children and other young persons are often cruel in their slighting remarks and slurring nicknames. The overweight child is shunned, ridiculed, omitted from games, parties because he or she is "too fat" or "could not keep up with the others."

These principles equally apply to adults. How many times in the corporate world do we see a promotion given to the candidate who is aesthetically more pleasing? Just think of how many overweight female news anchors you see on television, not many.

In addition to the obvious health hazards represented by being overweight, it is a handicap socially, economically, aesthetically, psychologically and occupationally.

Do not be in a hurry to permanently lose weight. Using self-hypnosis, for example, requires only a few minutes, but requires regular exposure until the subconscious is properly reprogrammed.

In applying self-hypnosis, a serious attitude and motivation are critical. This is not to imply straining towards your goal. Hypnosis is a relaxation method and any predisposed tension or anxiety will only retard your progress. Time also must be allowed for your suggestions to become incorporated within your subconscious.

My purpose in presenting the various regimens and exercises in this book is to train you to improve your outlook on life in general, along with your health. This new state of optimism and psychic empowerment will also assist you in losing weight permanently and naturally.

The only motivation that will ultimately push you to your goal is the belief that you can succeed for yourself. I am not advocating you make these changes to satisfy or patronize others, no matter how well-meaning and loving they may be. "To thine own self be true."

These methods require you making a permanent commitment to your health and your goal of leaner living. There is no such thing as quick fix for weight loss. You cannot stay lean if you slip back into your old eating habits. To achieve these goals you need to eat low-fat, high-carbohydrate, high-fiber foods from a variety of food groups.

Such practices as eating when you are physiologically hungry, eating slowly and savoring each bite, emphasizing high-fiber foods such as fruit, vegetables and grains and consuming cereal or low-fat bread products such as bagels instead of high-fat snack foods, are what I am referring to.

PERSONAL GROWTH

By far, the most important application of self-hypnosis is towards your own personal growth. As you grow spiritually your psychic empowerment (taking charge of your life) will enhance accordingly. Other areas where you can expect an increase are your self-image, creativity, resistance to stress, performance in any task, and ability to learn.

This creates a chain reaction. By improving the mind-body-spirit connection, you create a boundless, unstoppable momentum.

Your results will have practical applications. This won't mean much if you aren't happy.

In my Los Angeles office I see many wealthy, famous, and powerful people. They have everything they want, except for one thing: They are miserable. It may be difficult to comprehend how people with so many advantages could be so unhappy. These celebrity patients do not request my hypnotherapy services to brag about how great their life is. Who hasn't heard about dysfunctional, self-defeating behavior of the rich and famous?

Apply this to your own life. Remember that motivation and psychic empowerment are the most important qualities you can have. The rest is simply a matter of time and application. Solving your personal problem is an important component of your spiritual evolvement.

Be conscientious in your lifestyle and subconscious in reprogramming. Adopt a positive, optimistic, empowered and spiritual outlook and behavior and you will quickly see that you too can lose weight permanently and naturally.

1 Thomas Moore, *Care of the Soul* (New York: Harper Collins, 1992).
2 Ibid.
3 DiPietro et al., "Behavioral Risk Factor Surveillance Survey, 1989." *Intl Jnl Obesity 17* (1993) : 69-76.
4 O. Owens, "A reappraisal of caloric requirements in healthy women." *American Journal of Clinical Nutrition*, Volume 44 (1986): 1-19.
5 R. Heller and R. Heller, *The carbohydrate addict's diet: the lifelong solution to yo-yo dieting* (New York: Dutton, 1991).
6 B. Goldberg, *Soul Healing* (St. Paul: Llewellyn, 1996).
7 B. Goldberg, *New Age Hypnosis* (St. Paul: Llewellyn, 1998).

CPSIA information can be obtained at www.ICGtesting.com
Printed in the USA
LVOW122238290313

326735LV00001B/160/A